# LEAN WEBSITES

BY **BARBARA BERMES**

**WITHDRAWN**
UTSA LIBRARIES

## Lean Websites

by Barbara Bermes

Copyright © 2015 SitePoint Pty. Ltd.

**Product Manager**: Simon Mackie     **English Editor**: Ralph Mason

**Technical Editor**: Andrew Betts     **Cover Designer**: Alex Walker

Published by SitePoint Pty. Ltd.

48 Cambridge Street Collingwood
VIC Australia 3066
Web: www.sitepoint.com
Email: business@sitepoint.com

ISBN 978-0-9922794-6-2 (print)

ISBN 978-0-9941826-6-1 (ebook)
Printed and bound in the United States of America

## About Barbara Bermes

Barbara has been an ardent performance advocate and web technologist for many years, working on a variety of web projects, most recently for the Canadian Broadcasting Corporation. As an international speaker, a contributor to jsmanners, and the organizer of the Toronto Web Performance Meetup, Barbara shares her passion and knowledge of web performance with the community.

## About SitePoint

SitePoint specializes in publishing fun, practical, and easy-to-understand content for web professionals. Visit http://www.sitepoint.com/ to access our blogs, books, newsletters, articles, and community forums. You'll find a stack of information on JavaScript, PHP, Ruby, mobile development, design, and more.

*To you, who thinks she can't do it — you absolutely can!*

*Please trust and follow your heart.*

# Table of Contents

## Chapter 3   Measuring & Monitoring Performance . . . . . . . . . . . . 23

## Chapter 4   Performance Boot Camp Setup . . . . . . 57

## Chapter 5   Mastering Lean HTTP Requests

## Chapter 6   Producing Lean Web Assets: Part 1

## Chapter 7  Producing Lean Web Assets: Part 2 . . . . . . . . . . . . . . . . . . . . . . . . . . . . . . . . 135

## Chapter 12   Performance Cheat Sheet . . . . . . . . . . . 237

# Preface

We've grown into a very impatient society—a culture of "survival of the fastest". Waiting is not an option any more. Search engines like Google, Bing, and Yahoo are competing to offer the fastest and best search results. Ecommerce sites like Amazon, Target and Walmart are competing with innovative delivery methods like same-day delivery drones[1]. And our everyday life is increasingly moving towards an online life, where slowness is not acceptable. We expect to be able to do more and more online, and to do it quickly—from ordering food to buying goods, or even finding relationships. If a site feels slow, we'll probably complain to the site owner, our friends and on social media, and possibly not visit the site again, but move on to find alternatives.

Although Internet speeds have increased, websites are getting bigger and more complex by the year, and so they inevitably need to be powered by more powerful technologies to satisfy the impatient users of today. But why is the overall size of websites increasing? Are we getting lazy and taking current, high-speed infrastructures for granted, no longer caring about clean, lean and performant code?

Technology allows us to "go bigger", but maybe not necessarily be better when it comes to performance. Servers and Internet connections are getting more sophisticated, and as a result, we feel the need to keep filling them. However, this isn't the time to become lazy. This is the time to utilize the amazing tools that are available for making websites faster, and to learn how to improve user experience and satisfaction. Because nobody likes to wait.

The charts in Figure 1 and Figure 2, sourced from HTTP Archive, show the size and number of HTTP requests of websites, and how both measurements have increased over recent years:

---

[1] http://en.wikipedia.org/wiki/Delivery_drone

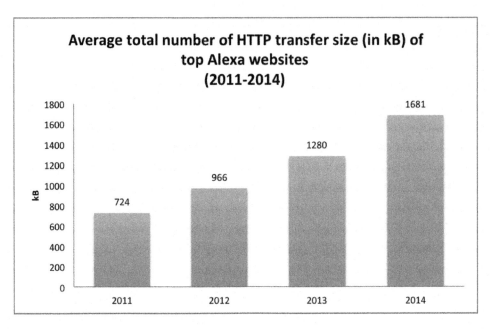

Figure 1. Increase in average website transfer size, 2011-2014

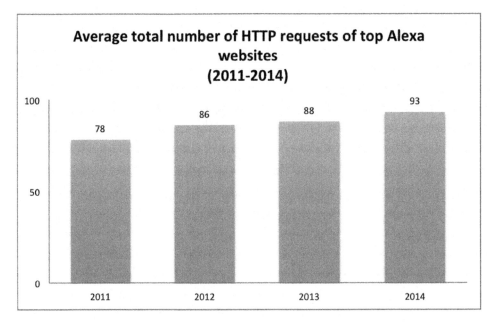

Figure 2. Increase in average number of HTTP requests per website, 2011-2014

From 2010 to 2014, the average total transfer size—basically the overall weight—of a website increased by 150%, compared to the total number of requests (all the assets of the website that need to be loaded), which only increased by around 16%. We can clearly see a trend towards more complex web applications. Our code needs to be performant to handle the rise of sophisticated applications. This book will show you how to make your websites leaner and faster.

### An Exercise Routine for Your Website

Throughout this book, you'll notice that I've used various references to exercise routines, notably the "Warm Up" and "Cool Down" sections in each chapter. Indeed, the title of this book, *Lean Websites*, also implies exercise. The primary reasoning behind that idea is that you'll want to make your sites slimmer in order to make them faster. However, additionally, by implementing the techniques discussed in this book over and over, like an exercise routine, you'll develop a web performance "muscle memory" that will become ingrained in your web development routine—establishing habits that will make building efficient, performant websites seem like second nature.

# Who Should Read This Book

This book assumes experience of web development, and familiarity with HTML, CSS, and JavaScript. Some back-end experience would be useful.

# Conventions Used

You'll notice that we've used certain typographic and layout styles throughout the book to signify different types of information. Look out for the following items:

## Code Samples

Code in this book will be displayed using a fixed-width font, like so:

```
<h1>A Perfect Summer's Day</h1>
<p>It was a lovely day for a walk in the park. The birds
were singing and the kids were all back at school.</p>
```

If the code is to be found in the book's code archive, the name of the file will appear at the top of the program listing, like this:

```
                                                            example.css
.footer {
  background-color: #CCC;
  border-top: 1px solid #333;
}
```

If only part of the file is displayed, this is indicated by the word *excerpt*:

```
                                                    example.css (excerpt)
  border-top: 1px solid #333;
```

If additional code is to be inserted into an existing example, the new code will be displayed in bold:

```
function animate() {
  new_variable = "Hello";
}
```

Where existing code is required for context, rather than repeat all the code, a vertical ellipsis will be displayed:

```
function animate() {
  ⋮
  return new_variable;
}
```

Some lines of code are intended to be entered on one line, but we've had to wrap them because of page constraints. A ➥ indicates a line break that exists for formatting purposes only, and should be ignored:

```
URL.open("http://www.sitepoint.com/blogs/2015/05/28/user-style-she
➥ets-come-of-age/");
```

## Tips, Notes, and Warnings

### Hey, You!

Tips will give you helpful little pointers.

### Ahem, Excuse Me ...

Notes are useful asides that are related—but not critical—to the topic at hand. Think of them as extra tidbits of information.

### Make Sure You Always ...

... pay attention to these important points.

### Watch Out!

Warnings will highlight any gotchas that are likely to trip you up along the way.

# Supplementary Materials

**http://www.learnable.com/books/webperf1/**
The book's website, which contains links, updates, resources, and more.

**https://github.com/spbooks/webperf1/**
The downloadable code archive for this book.

**http://community.sitepoint.com/**
SitePoint's forums, for help on any tricky web problems.

**books@sitepoint.com**
Our email address, should you need to contact us for support, to report a problem, or for any other reason.

# Acknowledgements

There are no words that can describe how thankful I am towards my family for supporting my career, and never making me feel guilty for leaving them. Thank you Papa, Anna, Kathy, Michael, my nephew Jan and nieces Antonia and Lisa, as well as all the beautiful family members who are not with us any more

My biggest thanks and appreciation goes out to Daniela, who has given me so much love. She was there when I was happy and ecstatic to be writing the book but also when I was down and exhausted, not knowing if the book would turn out the way

I (and the editors) wanted. Thank you for all the lost hours and weekends you had to sacrifice. Your ability to lift me up, and provide supporting and constructive feedback was invaluable.

Another big thanks goes out to Rebecca for always being available to proofread, and to comment on my second language adventures. I want to thank my "patchwork family" and life-long friend Alex for his great comments, love and support for keeping me going. Their constant support and encouragement was invaluable.

Thanks to SitePoint's Simon Mackie, and the extremely knowledgeable and honest Andrew Betts, for their constructive feedback, and for pushing me to form and shape the book as it is now.

Big thanks to my little friend Emilia for helping me focus and learn what matters in life. Babysitting her, and writing at the same time, was one of the nicest, most calming and productive activities during this journey. Thanks for the kisses and bedtime stories before my book writing night shifts began.

Thanks to all the great, smart and fun people in the web performance community for their knowledge and supportive camaraderie.

While many early mornings and late evenings have been spent on this book, not only the beautiful stars have always helped me continue but also my dear friends. I'm nothing without my friends (you know who you are), so the closing thanks goes out to them for letting me hide to write over several months, and for letting me be my true self, every day. Thanks to all of you for brightening my life, and for giving me a heart full of support, love, and laughter—every single day!

Thank you.

# Want to take your learning further?

Thanks for choosing to buy a SitePoint book. Do you want to continue learning? You can now gain unlimited access to courses and ALL SitePoint books at Learnable for one low price. Enroll now and start learning today! Join Learnable and you'll stay ahead of the newest technology trends: http://www.learnable.com.

# Performance Simply Matters

## A Lean Website

This book, *Lean Websites*, examines the causes behind bloated and slow websites, dissects which assets of your page are necessary, which are nice to have, and which are not necessary at all and can be removed to shed some weight. It will help you understand what causes websites to be slow, and how to look for efficiency while maintaining the quality originally envisioned for your site.

The title of the book includes the word **lean**. So what does the word mean?

"Lean" is used in this book to describe both the nature of the product we create and the process of creating it. Keeping a product lean means removing anything that might impede its performance. In the case of a website, this means keeping a clear focus on elements that add value to the site, and ensuring that these elements are optimized to provide the best possible user experience. Likewise, the more we practice building healthy, lightweight websites, the leaner and more efficient the process becomes—hopefully becoming part of our DNA when deploying sites.

But let's be clear up front: there's some bad news. From a performance perspective, there's *a lot* you can do wrong—and probably are doing wrong—when it comes to building websites! But hey, there's also good news: there are lots of relatively easy ways to fix those problems.

"The secret of getting ahead is getting started," as the saying goes. So let's get started!

# The Psychology of Speed

Why do people leave a website? There could be many reasons, such difficulty finding what they are looking for. But there's a good chance users leave a site because it feels too slow to load. In this section, I want to draw some attention to psychology, and how it plays a big role in our perception of speed and performance.

## What Is "Too Slow", and When Do Websites "Feel" Slow?

As psychologist Jeremy Dean points out, time doesn't fly when we are having fun[1]. When do we experience fun? Clearly, it's not when we have to wait. Who likes to wait, especially in this world of constant news and response? Nowadays, people desire instant satisfaction and have very little patience. Amazon offers one-day delivery; a cab shouldn't take longer than ten minutes to arrive. We've become a society where waiting is not acceptable anymore—especially when it comes to the online world. When we visit websites, if we don't get an instant response, a competitor's site is just a click away.

A watched pot never boils. Minutes drag when we are bored.[2]

The problem with discussing website speed is that the perception of speed is very subjective and very context specific. What feels slow to me might not feel slow, say, to my father or my grandmother. We all have different expectations. For this reason, Chapter 3 will help us to formulate a definition of "too slow" with real numbers and data.

---

[1] http://www.spring.org.uk/2011/06/10-ways-our-minds-warp-time.php
[2] http://www.theguardian.com/science/2013/jan/01/psychology-time-perception-awareness-research

# Maister's First Law of Service

David Maister, a former professor at the Harvard Business School, came up with a formula for the law of service. The formula—the outcome of several years of research—provides a measurement on how waiting for a specific service affects customers' perceptions of both the service provided and the actual product.

Maister's formula states that Satisfaction = Perception - Expectation.[3] In the context of web performance and serving content to site visitors, this formula raises the following questions:

- What was actually served and presented to the visitor, and did the content satisfy the user's goal?

- What was perceived by the visitor?

- What did the visitor actually expect?

## Satisfaction

Imagine a situation where you visit a page and a loading indicator slowly moves from 5% to 10%. You'll expect it to take a while to hit 100%. If the percentage unexpectedly begins to rise quickly to 95% and then 100%, you'll be satisfied and happy, because your perception exceeded your expectation. Conversely, if the loading indicator goes up slower than you expect, you'll experience an unpleasant feeling.

In a nutshell, website visitors are satisfied when their perception exceeds their expectation, and dissatisfied when the opposite occurs.

## Perception

We need to acknowledge that the perception of website speed is a *feeling*—something that is very subjective.

For example, perception refers to how fast the user *thinks* your website is, rather than how fast it *actually* is. Most of the time, that's almost more important than the actual speed of your website.

---

[3] http://faculty.haas.berkeley.edu/andy/blockhandouts/Queue%20Psychology.ppt

Generally, the perception of something being slow[4] carries negative associations—unpleasantness, boredom, irritation, confusion and so on. Speed, on the other hand, is associated with success, resulting in less frustration and irritation—especially where the user is kept informed of progress.

Given that your website's loading time can be perceived as slow, it's important to ensure that content is delivered as quickly as possible—or at least that, during any delay, the user is kept busy and distracted, so that the experience doesn't *feel* slow to them.

There's a great example[5] that illustrates the problem of perception. The Houston airport received a lot of complaints from passengers that it took too long to get their luggage. Instead of making the hard working airport personnel work even faster to get the luggage out, the airport decided to change the way passengers perceived the waiting time to pick up their luggage. They extended the distance from the arrival gate to the baggage claim sixfold. While the airport personnel were busy moving all the luggage to the baggage claim, passengers were kept busy by walking. The time for the bags to come out hadn't changed. However, as a result of perceived performance, complaints started dropping dramatically.

## Expectations

In the context of performance, when servicing customers, it's important to manage and care about their expectations. Disney has done a fabulous job in managing expectations so the customer receives a positive outcome in their amusement parks. They have lineups that show you the expected waiting times, with a rather pessimistic estimate, so that customers get to the front of the line in a much shorter time than predicted. As a result, the customer feels more positive.

So, how does this translate to servicing website visitors? We should set clear expectations by keeping them informed about the progress of their task. Show them the content they want to see in the fastest possible way; and, if waiting is required, show progress bars or other indicators to reassure them the website is still responding, and that they'll receive the content that they requested.

---

[4] http://www.slideshare.net/stoyan/psychology-of-performance

[5] http://www.nytimes.com/2012/08/19/opinion/sunday/why-waiting-in-line-is-torture.html?pagewanted=all&_r=0

### Respect

I'd like to mention "respect", as I believe it's an important factor in customer satisfaction. Ultimately, performance is about respect. Imagine you are made to stand in line for 20 minutes, only to find the cashier closing just before it's your turn to be served. Frustrating, right? Couldn't they have told you earlier? That's where respect comes into play: the greater the respect shown for customers, the more likely they are to experience satisfaction.

# Abandonment Rate: When Your Users Decide to Leave

We've all abandoned a service before. Standing in an unmoving line will make us impatient, until we give up and quit. We leave the queue and don't finish the task we actually wanted to accomplish. We experience frustration and disappointment. The same can happen with websites. If users consider your website helpful and fast, they'll stay and finish their task. Otherwise, they'll leave your site without completing their task. Therefore, the **abandonment rate** is probably the safest and most honest judgement you can get from your users on how satisfied they are with your service.

There are many statistics and case studies demonstrating that abandonment behavior of users is due to poor performance. Ecommerce websites are hit the hardest. Stiff competition forces site owners to pay close attention to speed and execution. If your shopping cart doesn't load fast enough, your users might just move to a competitor's site.

Here are some real-world statistics and numbers[6] that prove how important speed is in a world of invaluable instantness:

- Amazon calculated that a page load slowdown of just one second could cost them $1.6 billion in sales each year[7]

- Almost 40% of online shoppers abandon a website that takes more than 3 seconds to load (Gomez[8])

---

[6] http://www.webperformancetoday.com/2010/06/15/everything-you-wanted-to-know-about-web-performance/

[7] http://www.fastcompany.com/1825005/how-one-second-could-cost-amazon-16-billion-sales

[8] http://www.mcrinc.com/Documents/Newsletters/201110_why_web_performance_matters.pdf

- 79% of online shoppers will not return to a website after a disappointing experience due to poor performance (KissMetrics[9])

- A 1-second delay in page load time equals 11% fewer page views, a 16% decrease in customer satisfaction, and 7% loss in conversions (Aberdeen Group[10])

# Response Time

Perceived web performance involves how we, as humans, experience and respond to the performance of a system.

The following graph shows how different response times of systems effect our brain, and how our brain deals with them, resulting in different emotions:

| Instant | Slight perceptible delay | Perceptible delay | Mental context switch | Forget it, I'll leave |

100ms        300ms              1000ms          +10000ms

Figure 1.1. Perceived performance in milliseconds, and how our brain reacts[11]

- We feel **instant perception** around a **100ms** delay

- A **slight perceptible delay** occurs between **100ms and 300ms**

- We definitely feel a **perceptible delay** under **1000ms (1s)**

- After **1 second**, we feel that a **mental context switch** starts

- After **10 seconds** and more, the **abandon rate** goes up and the user tends to leave the site

---

[9] https://blog.kissmetrics.com/loading-time/?wide=1
[10] http://www.aberdeen.com/research/5136/ra-performance-web-application/content.aspx
[11] Source: Web Performance Today
[http://www.webperformancetoday.com/2014/07/16/eight-tricks-improve-perceived-web-performance/]
and High Performance Browser Networking
[http://chimera.labs.oreilly.com/books/1230000000545/ch10.html#SPEED_PERFORMANCE_HUMAN_PERCEPTION]

### Mental Context Switch

A **mental context switch** happens when the user abandons the original purpose of coming to the site. They most likely are no longer interested in finishing their initial task.

While each user will have a different tolerance for delay, we can expect a scale of perception for a *typical* user based on the data referenced above.

The research really outlines the need to avoid any kind of delay as much as possible. Ilya Grigorik, a web performance advocate at Google, calls it the 1000ms "time to glass" challenge[12]. In order to fully satisfy your user's expectation, you have around 1000ms for your content to travel from your server to the user's glass (screen).

If you want to achieve a fast experience for your users, you need to understand what aspects could harm such a goal.

# Speed Matters: Everybody Cares, Even Google

Making users happy when your site is responsive and fast, and reducing operational and server costs by serving fewer bytes over the wire, are not the only benefits of focusing on performance. Google has made it official[13] that their search ranking algorithm takes page speed seriously, organising search results on that basis. This goes back to a blog entry[14] Google posted in 2010, stating that "users place a lot of value in speed—that's why we've decided to take site speed into account in our search rankings."

This is especially important when you have to deal with a lot of competitor products and websites. Being faster than your competitors definitely puts you ahead of the curve when somebody is googling for a service that you offer.

The Alexa rank measures the popularity of a website against all the other websites on the Web. Alexa's metrics are based on page views and visitors to those sites.

---

[12] https://www.igvita.com/slides/2013/io-pagespeed.pdf
[13] http://www.thinkwithgoogle.com/articles/the-google-gospel-of-speed-urs-hoelzle.html
[14] http://googlewebmastercentral.blogspot.ca/2010/04/using-site-speed-in-web-search-ranking.html

Some research[15] has recently been done on top-ranked pages and their speed, investigating whether or not the popularity of a website correlates with the **Start Render** time. Start Render time will be discussed in more detail in Chapters 3 and 4, but for now, let's say it's a metric that records the time when the browser starts to "paint" content on the screen. It's a helpful measurement in the context of perceived performance. If users can "see" content, it makes them feel that the website is ready to be browsed. However, the Start Render time only indicates that the page content has *started* to load, so even if users can view content, they may not actually be able to interact with it yet.

# Cool Down

In this introductory chapter, we've looked at the relationship between psychology and performance, the perception of speed, and what it means to be slow.

We've looked at why it's important to tackle web performance and how this can be approached. The following chapters will present tools and techniques for improving the perceived performance of your site, and ultimately for producing lean websites in the future.

---

[15] http://bigqueri.es/t/are-popular-websites-faster/162

# User Experience and Performance

## Warm Up

In this chapter, you'll learn about the relationship between user experience and performance. A website's user experience depends on several different factors: design, accessibility, information architecture, usability, perception, and performance.

For the purposes of this book, we'll focus on information architecture, design, and performance, which should all go hand in hand. Performance should be incorporated at the early design stage, and not added as an afterthought. It starts with content organization and architecture. The goal of performant information architecture is to serve the content that your users are looking for, in the most convenient, easiest and fastest possible way. Improving performance is an important factor in winning satisfied customers.

We'll finish the chapter by discussing a practical technique for bridging the gap between information architecture, design and performance, which I call the "performance point system". In order to demonstrate the idea behind the performance point system, I'll apply it to a real-world website.

# UX Principles

"User experience encompasses all aspects of the end-user's interaction with the company, its services, and its products." — Jakob Nielsen

There are several principles you can follow to achieve good user experience. First of all, you want to make sure you know and understand the user's goal. You want to ask yourself why users are coming to your website. For example, the user goals of a shopping site such as Amazon, and of a public transit website, are very different. Whereas Amazon tries to persuade users to hang out for hours on their site, while making suggestions on similar products, a public transit website has another goal—to provide users with the train schedule as soon as possible. Once the user has the schedule information, they will most likely exit the site.

Now it's up to the UX team to make sure the site supports the goal. It's worth coming up with hypothetical user journeys to measure their completion time. In the case of Amazon, the UX team needs to figure out how to keep users on the site. Using cookies and logins to retrieve information from previous visits, Amazon will want to seduce users into staying on the page by pretending to know them—and, more importantly, their interests. In the example of the public transit page, you could measure how many steps it takes to find or download the schedule, or to display the fares.

All UX user journeys should be created with performance in mind. The team should lay out the journey so the user will perceive each step of their journey as easily and fast as possible. That's where information architecture and wireframing come in.

# Information Architecture and Wireframes

A big part of user experience is **information architecture**[1] (IA), which defines the structural design of shared information environments. It's the art and science of organizing and labeling websites, intranets, online communities and software to support usability and findability. IA can be illustrated in wireframes. A **wireframe**[2]

---

[1] http://iainstitute.org/en/learn/resources/what_is_ia.php
[2] http://en.wikipedia.org/wiki/Website_wireframe

is a visual guide that represents the skeletal framework of a website. It's basically your first step in outlining the website.

The goal of this part of the process is to plan out the user's journey and flow while they explore the website. It's a very important piece in the process of developing websites, and it sets the tone of the user's journey. Performance should be considered as part of this journey. Instead of fixing performance issues later, make performance part of the wireframing process. Making good performance choices during this step can save you a lot of time later.

# Design for Performance

After wireframing, the next step is the design process.

Web designers love to create beautiful and aesthetic web pages, and they have a perfectly good reason for doing so. Thoughtful design can make a site welcoming, enjoyable to use and memorable. Design is a big part of user experience, but what about performance? Every single image or extra font you put on the page will affect the performance of the site.

Our generation is impatient[3], and even if a website is aesthetically appealing, the user may leave if it's slow.

In her excellent book *Designing for Performance*[4], Lara Hogan states, "It's imperative that designers weigh the balance between aesthetics and performance to improve the end user experience."

Don't get me wrong, I'm all for design and aesthetics, but they have to be reasonable, and more importantly context sensitive. There's no need to show everybody the high-resolution version of an image if it's not needed. Be context sensitive, considerate, and respectful. Don't fill your page with unnecessary, heavy assets like images just because you don't know what else to put there.

---

[3] http://www.bostonglobe.com/lifestyle/style/2013/02/01/the-growing-culture-impatience-where-instant-gratification-makes-crave-more-instant-gratification/q8tWDNGeJB2mm45fQxtTQP/story.html
[4] http://shop.oreilly.com/product/0636920033578.do

> ### Speed as a Design Feature
>
> Instagram is one of the companies that really focuses on the symbiosis of design and speed. Their motivation[5] is to find solutions for how speed can be a design feature.

# Perceived and Preemptive Web Performance

Performance is part of user experience. Even if the actual performance of your site might be less than ideal, there are ways to trick users into thinking the site has better performance.

This involves perceived and preemptive web performance. While **perceived performance** defines how your user perceives, or feels about, the loading of your website, **preemptive web performance** deals with predicting what the user might want to load next, dispatching it in advance to cut down on loading time later. As we learned in Chapter 1, you don't want users to become bored while waiting for web content to load. A website feels fast if the user is presented with a responsive system and is kept informed of progress.

Following the "fake it till you make it" principle can help improve the perceived speed of a site. Some tricks that can make website visitors believe a website is responsive and speedy include:

- **Offline caching**: with many modern browsers now supporting this, it can be used to provide an illusion of performance. It has helped Instagram[6] create fast-feeling user experiences. Instead of waiting for the server to respond to a photo upload, the offline cache presents the photo the user just attempted to upload. Afterwards, the photo is actually sent to the server. If you pay attention to the loading spinner in your mobile browser, you can spot this trick yourself.

- **Presenting instant feedback and reporting progress**: let the user know how far along they are in their journey through your site.

- **Placing important functionality at the top of the page**: by displaying important content to users **above the fold** (ATF)—at the top of the page, so they don't have

---

[5] https://speakerdeck.com/mikeyk/secrets-to-lightning-fast-mobile-design
[6] http://www.fastcodesign.com/1669788/the-3-white-lies-behind-instagrams-lightning-speed

to scroll—increases perceived performance. There's much more on ATF in Chapter 5.

- **Avoiding too many steps**: minimize the number of hoops users have to go through to achieve their goal.

Preemptive strategies take this a step further, but require a lot more intelligence. An example[7] is Instagram's photo upload functionality. Before a user hits the upload button, the image is uploaded in the background, purely on the assumption that this is the user's eventual intention. But this approach is not always recommended. If users don't have a good data plan on their mobile devices and want to save bandwidth, for example, this could really annoy them if they didn't actually want to upload the photo after all.

### Implementing Preemptive Performance

Newer browsers have started to adopt the preemptive approach, supporting techniques such as the `prefetch` and `prerender` attributes that make the browser look ahead for resources that might be needed. Chapter 5 will discuss these attributes in more detail.

# The Performance Point System

Now that we've learned some basic IA, design, and performance approaches, I'd like to propose a practical technique to bridge IA and design with performance: the **performance point system.** This might be a fun and easy way to get started, especially when you work with a design team. The idea behind this point system is to give the pre-development, non-technical members of the team a simple way to understand what components of a website could be considered "heavy", and which elements promise better perceived performance.

It's about "divide and conquer", the process of breaking down problems into sub-problems of the same type, until the individual sub-problems become simple enough to be solved directly.

---

[7] http://java.dzone.com/articles/mobile-ux-refining-perceived

We can break down the visual elements of the wireframe into measurable performance modules. We can then move them around and arrange them to accomplish not only an intuitive information architecture, but also a positive user experience.

Each module gets a number assigned, which defines its performance impact. At the end of the wireframing process, the numbers are summed to reveal a score. The lower the number, the better the expected performance.

This approach suggests that you don't have to *starve* your website by following performance patterns. A lean website in the context of this book does not refer to a website that is lacking any information or interaction. It only means that the website has been created with the concept of applying and following web performance paradigms, which I'll explore in more detail in later chapters.

## Measurable Performance Modules

A **measurable performance module** (MPM) describes a simplified and single performance unit in a wireframe. Its main purpose is to help non-technical members of the design and content team understand each module's performance impact to the overall website.

This might not be the most scientific translation of perceived performance, but it's useful for getting everybody on the same page during the early wireframing and design stages of a project:

| Module | Points | Description |
|---|---|---|
| Low impact | 1 | Small images, mostly static content and simple graphics, interaction elements like buttons and text fields. |
| Medium impact | 2 | Medium-sized images and simple scripts. |
| High impact | 6 | Large images and third-party scripts loading either heavy JavaScript or |

| Module | Points | Description |
|--------|--------|-------------|
|        |        | both JavaScript and images (such as adverts). |

Sit down with your design team, take a pencil, and start marking MPMs in the wireframe. Based on the table above, try to identify what modules on the wireframe represent low, medium or high performance impacts. This will be useful for the designer who creates a design from these wireframes, but also for the developer who must plan out the critical rendering path. (The critical rendering path—which we'll discuss in much more detail in Chapter 5—describes the code and resources required to render the initial view of a page.)

The end goal of this exercise is to have the entire team focused on getting the content to load and display as efficiently as possible.

Let's try this out on a real-world website.

# Case Study: Time Magazine Website

The following case study is used to show you how you can improve the wireframing process by applying MPMs to the site.

Let's take a look at the Time Magazine website:

Figure 2.1. The Time Magazine website loading

We can see, in the "filmstrip" in Figure 2.5 above, that the main story image only appears after around six seconds. There is no visible content prior to that. I've broken this down further into simple wireframes to illustrate how the site, above the fold, looks at various points in time as the site is being loaded.

Let's have a closer look at the current order:

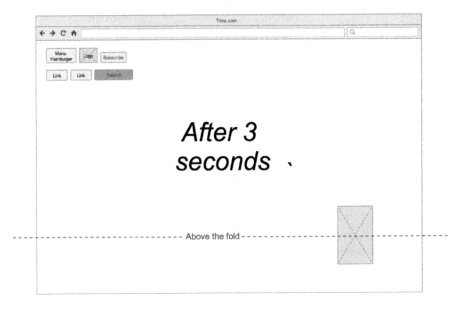

Figure 2.2. After 3 seconds, we only see the menu and the magazine image

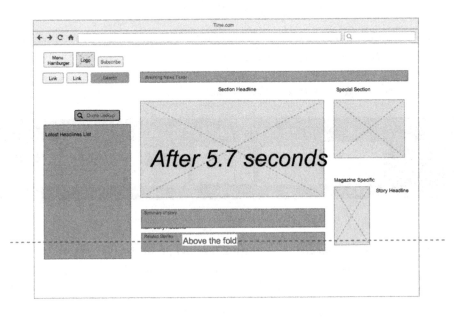

Figure 2.3. After 5.7 seconds, other important pieces are being loaded

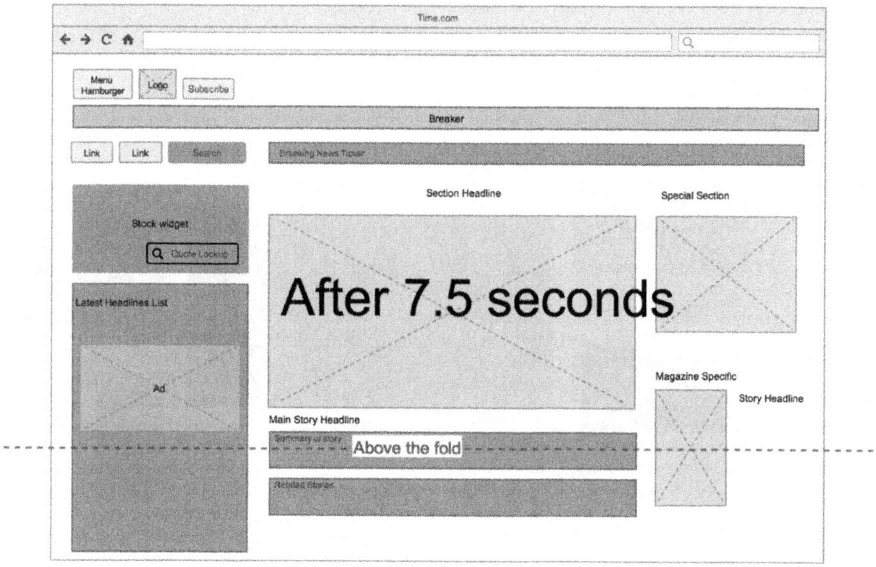

Figure 2.4. *After 7.5 seconds, most of the visible content above the fold has been loaded*

There is room for improvement, especially if our goal is to show the top story element as soon as possible.

## Current Performant Order Based on MDMs

Let's see how we can apply the point and order system to the wireframe.

The wireframe shown in Figure 2.5 was sketched based on one of the most common screen sizes[8] of today: 1366x768px. If you know your visitors' most used screen size, sketch it out based on that:

---

[8] http://www.w3schools.com/browsers/browsers_display.asp

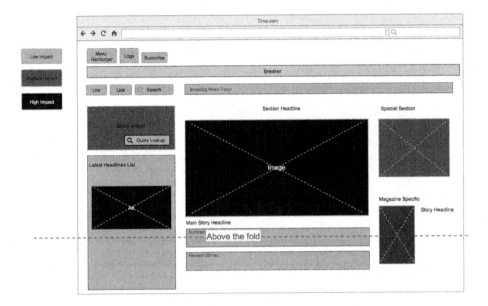

Figure 2.5. The Time.com website sketched out in wireframe

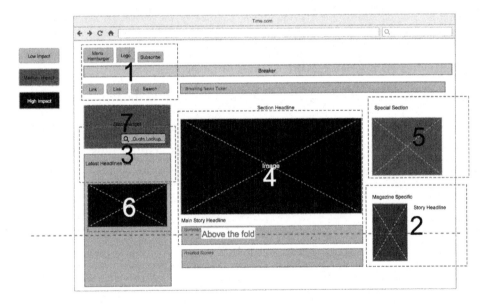

Figure 2.6. Time.com wireframe, including MPMs with order of appearance

I plotted the MPMs onto the wireframe in the image above, indicated by the dotted boxes. The number in each box describes the order in which each MPM appears on the screen. For example, the menu box was loaded first.

Here's the above the fold count of each MPM, categorized as low impact, medium impact, and high impact:

| Count | Module | Score |
|-------|--------|-------|
| 10 | Low impact | 10 |
| 2 | Medium impact | 4 |
| 2 | High impact | 12 |
| **14** | **Total** | **26** |

By checking the file sizes of each MPM, you can assess each MPM's impact. As mentioned before, this is mainly intended to bring design and developers together to quickly sketch out performance impacts of the different content modules. It lets you easily determine elements that might be too heavy to present above the fold.

## Suggested Performant Order based on MDMs

By making some adjustments to the site, we should be able to improve perceived performance. Although Time.com uses progressive JPEGs for their main story image, it seems that the image doesn't get the early attention it needs. Something in the code seems to be blocking its rendering, so that a user only sees it after 5.7 seconds.

Even if the main news image is classified as a high impact module, I would argue that, in this case, it is important to load this image as early as possible. So my proposed performant wireframe for Time.com could look like Figure 2.7:

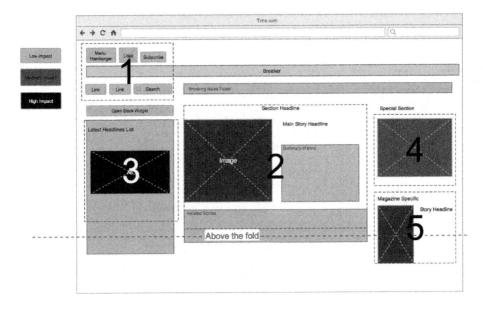

Figure 2.7. A performant wireframe for Time.com

Here is a new ATF count of MPMs, based on my changes:

| Count | Module | Score |
|-------|--------|-------|
| 12 | Low impact | 12 |
| 3 | Medium impact | 6 |
| 1 | High impact | 6 |
| **16** | **Total** | **24** |

I decreased the image height and width of the main story image, placing more context next to the image by aligning the headline and description to the right. I also replaced the stock data widget with a CTA button that the user has to press. Only when pressed will the stock data be loaded, which will somewhat reduce the ATF load time.

I also added some loading number priorities into the wireframe, so the developers will know where to put their focus when planning out the critical rendering path (which is a topic we'll discuss later).

If you're not sure which widgets and elements should be either removed or moved down below the fold, verify if those widgets and elements are actually used by your visitors. And if you decide that a heavy image (high impact MPM) should be placed above the fold, make sure to balance the performance budget with other low and medium impact modules.

A performant wireframe is not enough to make your website feel fast, but it's an excellent start on your journey to a lean website.

# Cool Down

In this chapter, we covered the following topics:

- ways to take performance into consideration and plan it out, early on

- how to "fake" a fast website

- the importance of perceived performance

- the idea of a performance point system and MDMs

One of the most important rules for performance is quantifying whether performance is good or bad. While *perceived* performance is an important aspect of web performance, the *actual* performance of the site is important too—and that can only be determined by measuring and monitoring. You can't improve something that you haven't measured first. The next chapter will introduce you to several important metrics, techniques and tools for measuring and monitoring site performance.

# Measuring & Monitoring Performance

## Warm Up

In the effort to improve something—be it a website or other product—it helps to be able to measure progress. Without effective measurement, it's hard to determine if something has improved or gotten worse. Fortunately, there are many tools at our disposal for testing and monitoring your website's performance. That's the focus of this chapter.

## Measuring Performance

In this section, we'll look at several tools for measuring and monitoring web performance.

### HTTP Archive: Tracking Performance Trends

HTTP Archive[1] is a free, online service that crawls the top 1 million Alexa websites to collect data on how these websites are built. You can use it to explore trends such as page sizes, load time, content delivery network (CDN) usage, distribution

---

[1] http://httparchive.org

of different content types (such as images, JavaScript and so on), and many other stats[2].

Here's an example of the interesting data the HTTP Archive presents:

▪ **Total transfer size and total requests**: the overall website page size is consistently growing. From 2012 to 2014, the page size went up by around 38%:

| Year (August 1) | Total transfer size[3] | Increase over previous year in % |
|---|---|---|
| 2012 | 1124 | - |
| 2013 | 1532 | 27 |
| 2014 | 1821 | 16 |

*HTTP Archive stats: Average Total Transfer Size and Total Requests from August 2012–14 for a single Top Alexa website*

▪ **JavaScript transfer size**: with all the trending JavaScript web applications, it's no wonder that JavaScript transfer size increased by more than 100%, from 113Kb in 2011 to around 289Kb in 2014.

▪ **Image formats**: the HTTP Archive can help you answer questions like "What's the most common image type used?" As you can see, the answer is JPEG:

---

[2] http://httparchive.org/interesting.php
[3] http://httparchive.org/about.php#bytesTotal

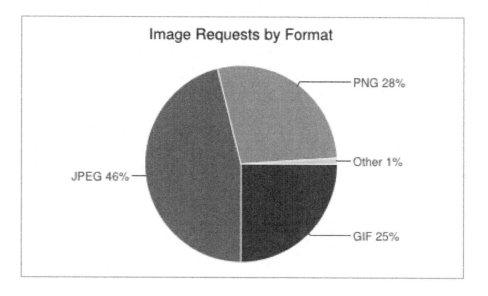

Figure 3.1. Image requests by format

Data of this kind is useful for understanding how your site compares with current standards.

The image below shows stats[4] from Time.com. If you're a news corporation, you might want to compare your site's stats with these. You can spot trends here. For example, Time.com seems to have reduced image file sizes as well as requests, which might indicate a trend in website optimization:

---

[4] http://httparchive.org/viewsite.php?pageid=17936268*

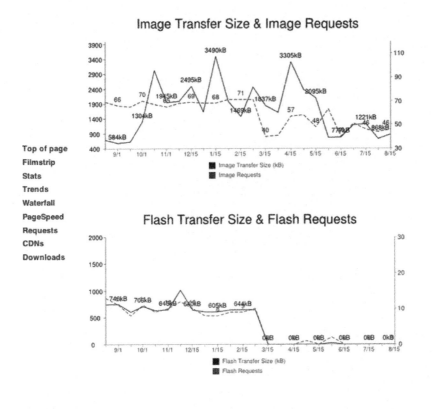

Figure 3.2. HTTP Archive's data for Time.com

The HTTP Archive provides a great introduction to the world of performance trends—answering many of the questions you or others in your company might have. It can also help your team focus on a specific direction. For example, if you're thinking of using a specific image format or following a particular trend, the HTTP Archive can help to back up that decision.

## Useful Performance Tools

There are many different tools available for measuring website performance, including commercial products like New Relic[5], Keynote[6] or Neustar[7]. Before you shell

---

[5] http://newrelic.com/application-monitoring

[6] http://www.keynote.com/

[7] http://www.neustar.biz/

out money for a tool, though, it's worth trying open source tools such as your browser and WebPagetest[8]. In this section, we'll look at what you can do with both of these.

## Browser-based Developer Tools

The quickest and easiest way to measure the performance of your site is to start with the developer tools of your preferred browser. Most browsers offer built-in developer tools that you can use to check your site's code and monitor its performance. Hit **Ctrl + Shift + I** on Windows, and **Cmd + Opt + I** on Mac in your browser to bring up the developer tools.

Figure 3.3 shows an example of the sitepoint.com website, opened in the Firefox developer tool's **Network** tab.

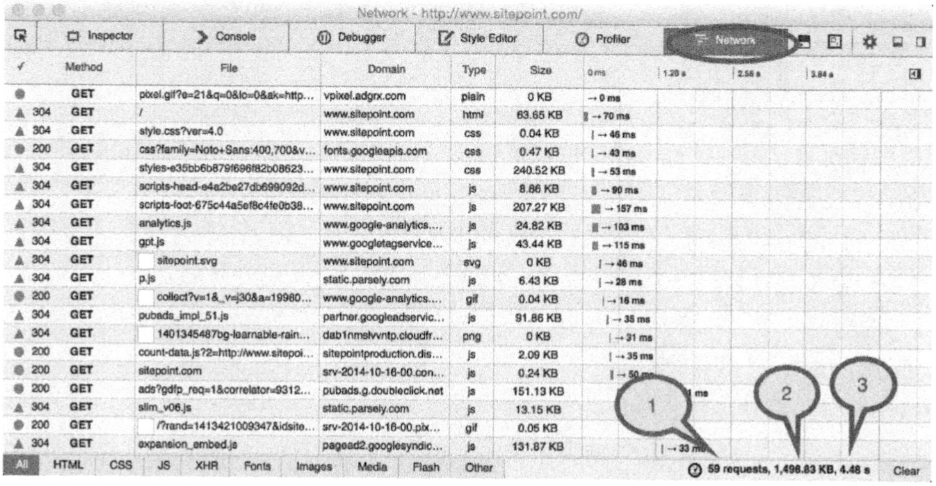

Figure 3.3. sitepoint.com stats shown in Firefox developer tools

At the bottom right of the image, we can see the following information:

1. the browser had to send 59 HTTP requests to render the page

2. the total page size is 1,498.83 kilobytes

3. the page took 4.48 seconds to fully load in the browser

---

[8] http://www.webpagetest.org

Other browsers offer even more functionality. Google's Chrome development team has been adding useful features to Chrome's developer tools. One of the additions is the **Timeline** tab, providing you with the entire overview of where most time is spent when loading a page (see Figure 3.4).

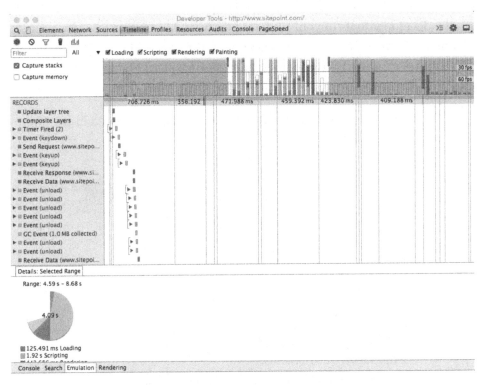

Figure 3.4. sitepoint.com stats viewed in Chrome's **Timeline** tab

Using this tool, you can select a range in time that you want to analyze. You can further drill down into each part of the rendering process. You can find out when most of the script execution is happening by looking at the yellow colored distribution.

The **Audits** tab lets you analyze the page while it loads, shown in Figure 3.5. The tool also provides you with suggestions on how to improve the performance of the page.

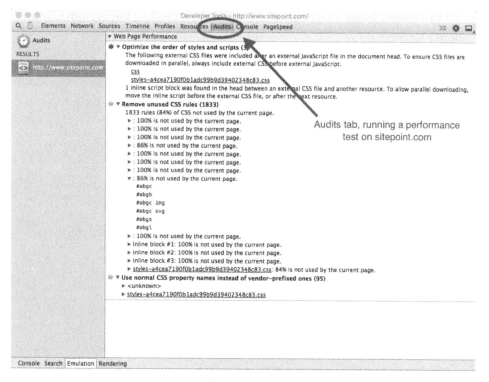

Figure 3.5. sitepoint.com analyzed in Chrome's Audits tab

# Resource Waterfall

Optimizing performance is about knowing how and when to load assets and avoiding any blocking of content: that's where the **resource waterfall** comes in handy.

Most of the performance tools I've mentioned so far include a resource waterfall (accessible via the **Network** tab in the developer tools of your browser). You got a glimpse of the resource waterfall when we looked at the basic information about sitepoint.com in Firefox's Network tab previously. So why is this view so important? Each web page consists of HTTP transactions (requests and responses). Bundled together, these make a website appear in your browser. They comprise the assets and resources of your website. The easiest way to visually represent all these HTTP requests is to plot them onto a so-called "waterfall". The reason why the resources are aligned in a waterfall is because the browser can't download all the resources at once. The browser follows rules for downloading each component, either in parallel or sequentially.

The image below shows an example of a resource waterfall, taken from Chrome's developer tools:

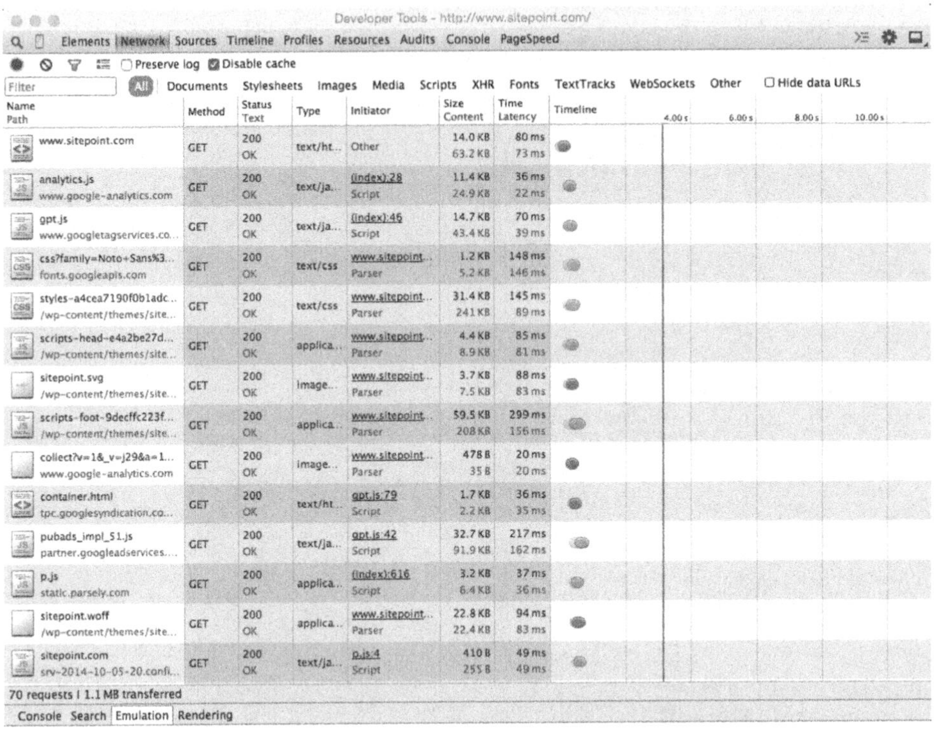

Figure 3.6. sitepoint.com's resource waterfall in Chrome's developer tools

# WebPagetest

My favorite performance tool is WebPagetest[9] (WPT), a free, online resource created and maintained by Patrick Meenan. (WPT data forms the backbone of the HTTP Archive, whose monthly runs analyze and process the WPT results of the top Alexa websites.)

Below is a screenshot illustrating a WPT test. Type in the URL you want to test, and you're presented with a performance analysis, including a detailed waterfall:

---

[9] http://www.webpagetest.org/

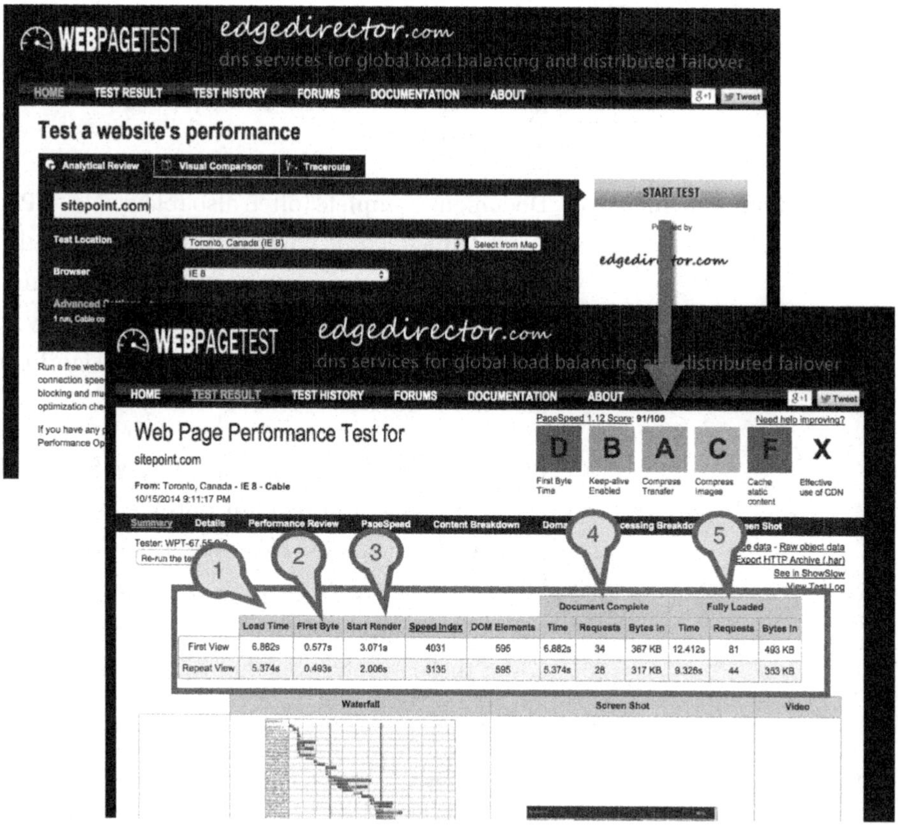

Figure 3.7. sitepoint.com stats in WPT

In addition to the data available in most browser developer tools (total requests, total page size, and page load time), WPT provides several other important metrics:

**1. Load Time**

The **Load Time** is measured as the time from the start of the initial navigation until the beginning of the window load event (`onload`).

**2. First Byte**

The **First Byte** time is measured as the time from the start of the initial navigation until the first byte of the base page is received by the browser (after following redirects).

**3. Start Render**

The **Start Render** time is the first point in time that content starts to appear in the browser. This could even just be the background color, or the logo at the top corner of the page. The Start Render time is also plotted in the waterfall as a green line, which ideally should appear as early as possible.

**4. Document Complete (or Page Load Time)**

**Document Complete** (often also referred to as **Page Load Time**) records when the initial page loading process is complete. You can also capture this moment via JavaScript's `window.onload()` event. For heavy websites, page load can take significant amount of time.

Images and content not pushed via JavaScript will be fully loaded at this point in time, including non-visible elements. However, if JavaScript is being used to trigger the push of content (via Ajax calls, for example), they may not be included. To count these events, you should be looking at the "Fully Loaded" figures.

**5. Fully Loaded**

**Fully Loaded** time occurs when all assets of the page have been loaded, including any activity that is triggered by JavaScript after the main content has loaded.

We'll look at more features of WPT later in this chapter and throughout the rest of the book.

# Dedicated Perceived Performance Metrics

Let's take a quick look at a few important perceived performance metrics that we'll refer to frequently in this book.

## Above Fold Time

The **Above Fold Time** (AFT) is an important metric that can be used to quantify the perceived performance of a website.

AFT is a measure of the time required to fully render just the part of the page users can initially see on their screen. The browser may still be loading assets further down the page below the fold. AFT can provide a better indication of how the user experiences performance than page load time (PLT). (In Chapter 4, we'll look at some examples of how the PLT can misrepresent perceived performance.)

## Speed Index

**Speed Index** was added to WebPagetest in 2012, and describes "the average time at which visible parts of the page are displayed[10]". The results are presented in milliseconds. The smaller the number, the better the site's performance.

Speed Index data can be used for A/B testing or general competitor comparison. Here are some examples:

| Website | Speed Index |
| --- | --- |
| facebook.com | 3524 |
| twitter.com | 2604 |
| sitepoint.com | 1342 |
| time.com | 10784 |

### A/B Testing

**A/B testing** involves presenting different users with two different versions (A and B) of your site. This process lets you compare the results between the two versions.

## PageSpeed

Google's answer to Speed Index is the **PageSpeed** score. It goes from 0 to 100 points, where a higher score is better. Google considers[11] a score of 85 to be a page that is performing well. The PageSpeed score can be obtained by running the PageSpeed Insights[12] tool on your page:

| Website | PageSpeed |
| --- | --- |
| facebook.com | 99 |
| twitter.com | 99 |

---

[10] https://sites.google.com/a/webpagetest.org/docs/using-webpagetest/metrics/speed-index
[11] https://developers.google.com/speed/docs/insights/about
[12] https://developers.google.com/speed/pagespeed/insights/

| Website | PageSpeed |
| --- | --- |
| sitepoint.com | 95 |
| time.com | 82 |

As you can see from the results of both performance tests above, PageSpeed and Speed Index seem not to match up fully with their judging criteria. While Speed Index focuses mostly on the ATF visibility and interactivity, Page Speed[13] also factors in the time it takes to load the page fully.

# Anatomy of an HTTP Transaction

Let's have a closer look at how each asset of a page is loaded.

Each item in the resource waterfall represents a network transaction, also called an HTTP transaction. An HTTP transaction describes the process of a client making a single request for HTTP content. When we talk about HTTP content, we normally refer to anything that can be received by the browser, in so-called content types.

**Content types** can be scripts, images, HTML, text, Flash, Excel or Word documents etc.—basically anything that can be served to, and displayed by, the browser. Any other content type that is not supported and can't be displayed will be offered as a download. The various content types are color-coded in the waterfall, as we saw previously.

In Figure 3.8 you can find a snippet of a WPT waterfall view for Time.com:

---

[13] https://developers.google.com/speed/docs/insights/about

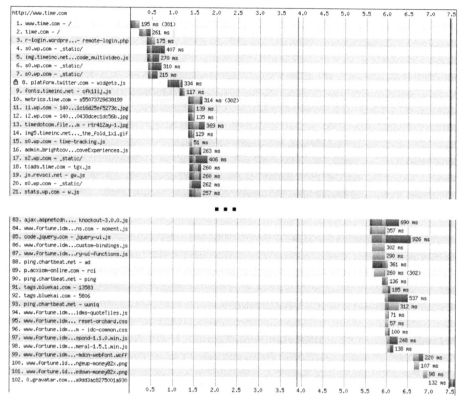

Figure 3.8. a WPT waterfall view for Time.com

Let's look at a particular asset in the waterfall: the Twitter widget.

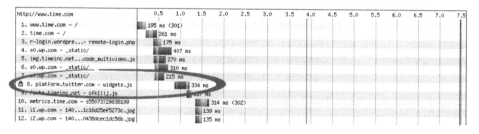

Figure 3.9. A Twitter JavaScript file being loaded very early on in the process of loading the page

Overall, it took the browser 334ms to load this file. The transaction shown in this waterfall consists of five different bars, each color-coded. The third one is the longest. This bar shows the time that was spent for the SSL negotiation.

So what does that all mean? Why did this event take the longest amount of time? And what do the other bars represent? Let's take a closer look. The image below breaks down this HTTP transaction:

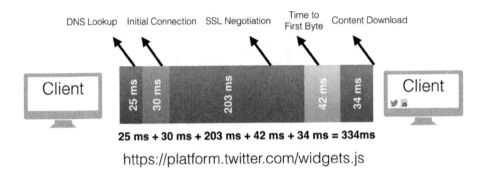

Figure 3.10. A closer look at an HTTP transaction in the waterfall

Let's examine these from the left to right.

**DNS Lookup**

**DNS** stands for Domain Name System. During the DNS lookup, the browser attempts to look up the domain of the asset it is trying to load. Each human-friendly URL has a computer-friendly IP address. You can use both in your browser. For example, www.sitepoint.com maps to 54.221.218.251.

There are many variables that can cause a delay[14] during this event.

**Initial Connection**

The **initial connection** occurs when the client and server perform a "handshake" to start communicating with each other over Transmission Control Protocol (TCP). The browser basically says "Hello, I want to request some stuff, are you available?" and the server says "Yes, I'm here, send away."

So what could cause a delay for this event? Each party needs to wait until the other party "has spoken". The

---

[14] https://www.igvita.com/posa/high-performance-networking-in-google-chrome/

server can't send anything until the browser has received the "Yes, I'm here, send away."

The travel time to communicate from sender to receiver is governed by speed of light limitations: the further they are apart from each other, the longer it will take to set up the TCP connection.

**SSL Negotiation**

**Secure Socket Layer** (SSL) enables secure communication. It's a protocol for encrypting information over the Internet (using https:// instead of http://). HTTPS in the scheme instructs the browser to perform a secure handshake.

### SSL or TLS?

SSL[15] was developed by Netscape Communications Corporation in 1994 to secure transactions over the World Wide Web. You've probably seen SSL in combination with TLS, sometimes even referred to as SSL/TLS. TLS stands for Transport Layer Security. SSL is the predecessor of TLS. The Internet Engineering Task Force standardized the SSL protocol, and named it TLS.

The differences[16] between TLS and SSL 3.0 are not dramatic, but they are significant enough to prevent interoperability between TLS 1.0 and SSL 3.0.

This event is about negotiation between two parties (the browser and the server). Each SSL negotiation over HTTPS requires a new TCP connection, including the process of a secure key exchange[17], making it more computationally expensive. However, modern hardware[18] has been able to absorb this disadvantage. Also, once negotiation has

---

[15] http://technet.microsoft.com/en-ca/library/cc784450.aspx
[16] https://www.ietf.org/rfc/rfc2246.txt
[17] http://publib.boulder.ibm.com/tividd/td/TRM/GC32-1323-00/en_US/HTML/admin231.htm
[18] http://chimera.labs.oreilly.com/books/1230000000545/ch04.html#TLS_COMPUTATIONAL_COSTS

been completed, the same connection can be used for any request to the same origin.

**Time to First Byte**

**Time to First Byte** (TTFB) occurs after the TCP handshake has successfully been executed, and after the browser and server have started talking to each other—when the first byte is actually sent to the browser.

This metric also represents latency. The bigger the green bar, the higher the latency. Depending on your location and/or the device you're using, you will notice smaller or bigger latency.

### Latency

Latency is the time it takes for the content to be requested by, and sent to, your browser. Latency can vary. It is affected by the distance the data has to travel and the medium that conducts it. You experience higher latency particularly on mobile networks[19]. Why? The radio of your device needs to find the closest tower to establish a connection. If the device is idle, it can take even longer.

TTFB comprises two factors: the actual physical distance from the browser to the server, and the processing time of the server. It can be summed up in the following formula: TTFB = Round trip network latency + back-end processing time.

Research[20] that tested around 300 uncached websites showed the largest web page load time component to be TTFB, followed by DNS lookup, connection time, and download time. Even for cached websites, TTFB was still the biggest load time component, followed by connection

---

[19] https://www.igvita.com/2012/07/19/latency-the-new-web-performance-bottleneck/

[20] http://www.websiteoptimization.com/speed/tweak/time-to-first-byte/

time, download time and DNS lookup. Hence it's worth focusing on optimizing TTFB.

If the TTFB is slow, other metrics will suffer from this delay, creating a chain reaction.

**Content Download**    This event occurs when the asset you requested actually starts to show up in your browser. You sometimes can guess by looking at the length of the blue bar how big the asset actually is. Images, for example, tend to have a bigger blue bar. The bigger the blue bar, the larger the actual asset, and hence the more time it takes to be sent over the wire.

Minimizing the file size of the asset is key to optimizing the amount of time spent on Content Download. Chapters 6 and 7 will present ways to optimize content such as images, JavaScript and HTML files.

# Unpredictable Side Effects: Connection Speed, Bandwidth and Latency

While we can influence the performance factors mentioned above, those we'll discus in this section are mostly beyond our control, but are still important to keep in mind when developing lean websites.

## Bandwidth and Latency

It's important to consider your users' average bandwidth (connection speed)—which varies a lot between regions—when developing your website. The greater your users' bandwidth, the faster they're likely to retrieve your website.

Akamai's State of the Internet Report[21] contains a lot of great information about service providers, connection speeds by region, and mobile browser usage data:

| Region | Q1 2014 Average Mbps |
|--------|----------------------|
| Global | 3.9 |

---

[21] http://www.akamai.com/dl/akamai/akamai-soti-q114.pdf?WT.mc_id=soti_Q114

| Region | Q1 2014 Average Mbps |
|--------|----------------------|
| South Korea | 23.6 |
| Japan | 14.6 |
| Hong King | 13.3 |
| Switzerland | 12.7 |
| Netherlands | 12.4 |
| Latvia | 12 |
| Sweden | 11.6 |
| Czech | 11.2 |
| Finland | 10.7 |
| Ireland | 10.7 |

However, while bandwidth will likely improve in years to come, the latency that comes with it is not an easy problem to solve. Improving latency requires updates and enhancements—such as shorter cables through the oceans.

## Last Mile Latency

**Last mile latency** refers to the latency between your request and your Internet service provider (ISP). Although you may think most of the latency comes from the travel time between the cabling from continent A to B, it's actually on the way from your browser to your ISP where most of the latency bottleneck resides. This latency depends on the cabling from the end user's house to the provider, the technology being deployed, and the time of the day. Picking a provider based on these criteria will help to reduce latency for the end user. However, this is something you can't much influence as a website owner.

`traceroute` is a command line tool for measuring latency (for example, between you and your ISP). Here's an example:

```
traceroute to bbinto.me (23.229.170.160), 64 hops max, 52 byte
↪packets
1  7.11.164.201 (7.11.164.201)  22.272 ms  8.525 ms  8.197 ms
2  7.11.164.201 (7.11.164.201)  7.846 ms  11.971 ms  33.085 ms
3  209.148.243.105 (209.148.243.105)  24.445 ms  13.891 ms  11.978
↪ms // my ISP
```

```
...
13 be38.trmc0215-01.ars.mgmt.phx3.gdg (184.168.0.69)  100.097 ms
➡67.337 ms  74.092 ms
```

Line #3 shows the latency to my ISP, measured three times, ranging from around 12ms to 25ms. The first column describes the hops that the request has to "go through" to get to bbinto.me. It took 13 hops to get to bbinto.me: line #13 describes the GoDaddy server, the final destination.

# Monitoring Performance

So far, we've looked at some of the tools for measuring site performance. In this section, we'll focus on two techniques for monitoring site performance. The first, known as "synthetic testing", involves devising our own discrete tests. The second, known as "real user monitoring", involves studying actual end user behavior.

## Synthetic Measurements

**Synthetic** testing is the most common and controllable measurement tool available to developers. As opposed to real user monitoring, synthetic testing is done by you and is in your control. You decide when and how to run a test on your website. You can choose the specific conditions, such as the browser, network condition and/or geographical location.

You can use the free tools we've already discussed to make conduct synthetic tests—tools such as WebPagetest, PageSpeed Insights, or even your browser's developer tools.

### WebPagetest

We briefly discussed WPT earlier in this chapter. Let's look at some of its other features that enable us to perform synthetic tests on our sites.

Figure 3.11 shows an overview of its main functionality:

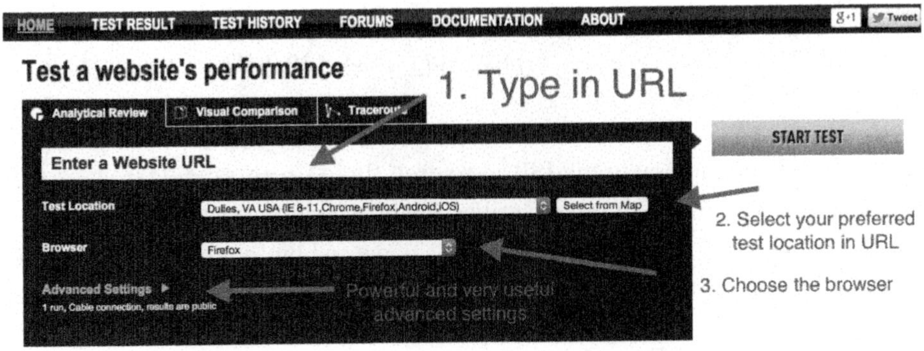

Figure 3.11. Basic view of the WPT interface, waiting for your input

The input is split into two sections—the basic information, such as the URL to test, and the advanced settings, such as defining how many times the test should run.

Let's first look at the basic settings:

- **Test Location**: choose the geographical location you want to get performance results for. This might be where most of your visitors come from, or even where barely any of your visitors come from. You might also choose a location based on complaints you've received—say from visitors in a country where the experience was poor.

- **Browser**: you can choose from a wide selection of browsers, including several mobile versions.

There are many different options you can choose under the **Advanced Settings**. For example, **Connection** lets you define exactly what connection speed should be used to test the URL, the **Repeat View** helps you review the site's performance with and without caching. The **Number of Tests to Run** helps you find the average of all runs combined. You can also record the test as a video, labeled as you like. If the site to be tested needs authentication, you can use the **Auth** tab to fill in the required credentials.

Figure 3.12 shows the **Advanced Settings**:

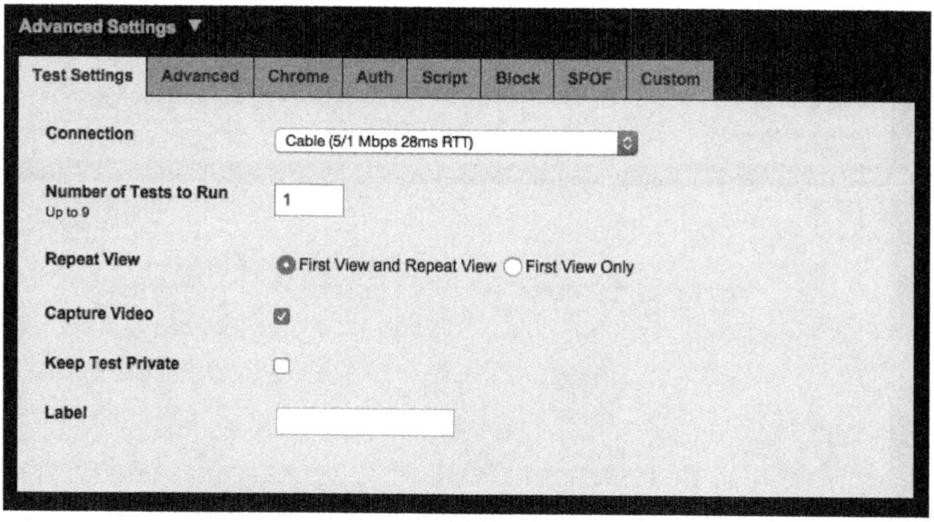

Figure 3.12. WPT's **Advanced Settings** interface

## Result Page

The WebPagetest result page provides a wealth of performance data—such as an ATF filmstrip, an evaluation of how many bytes are coming from third-party scripts as opposed to your own domain, and details of when the CPU time of the browser hit its peak.

As an example, I typed in Time.com with the location of Dulles, VA with Firefox on a cable connection as my test scenario. The following figure shows the corresponding result:

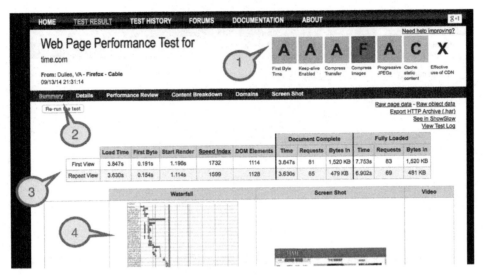

Figure 3.13. WPT result page for Time.com

Considering each of the numbered items in this screenshot in turn:

1. The grading area (top right) gives you a brief overview of how the site performs. The more greens and A's there are, the better.

2. There are several views to check out: the **Summary** tab gives you a brief but sufficient overview of the performance of the tested website.

3. The table has a breakdown of the most important metrics. We discussed most of them earlier. The two rows contain data collected in the first run (or test)—assuming the site has not been visited before (**First View**)—and the second test run (**Repeat View**). The second run reveals whether or not the site is utilizing caching (and if so, how it's doing so).

4. The rest of the result page includes waterfalls and screenshots illustrating the path your website has taken to render itself. The waterfall is color coded to help you understand where each asset spent most of its time loading.

5. There are some additional tools (not pictured) that you can utilize, such as exporting the test results in HAR or CSV formats for further investigation.

## What's HAR?

The official format of HTTP Archive files is called HAR. It's a JSON format that provides an easy way of exchanging network waterfalls (see below), saving you from having to share screenshots. HAR is a file format that can be exported and imported into many other useful tools[22].

## WPT's Waterfall

In my opinion, WPT's waterfall is the best available tool for investigating performance issues—providing much more information than those included in browser developer tools.

## Domain and Content Breakdown

The domain and content breakdown is very useful for evaluating the impact of third party scripts, and identifies right away what type of content occupies most of your bytes and requests.

## Get Yourself In Line

If you run many tests on the public WebPagetest instance, and depending on the time of the day, you will notice it can get really busy. Your test runs might end up in the queue next to many other tests from other users. If you feel your tests can't always wait, I would suggest you consider installing your own WPT instance[23]. It definitely gives you more flexibility and freedom when running tests. Otherwise, you'll need to wait in line, until your performance test is called by the WPT engine. Another advantage of having your own instance is that you can test websites before deployment.

## Unique ID

Each WPT run has a unique ID that you can always reference back to and review in the browser at a later point, such as http://www.webpagetest.org/result/140721_5F_1KP/.

---

[22] https://gist.github.com/igrigorik/3500508

[23] https://sites.google.com/a/webpagetest.org/docs/private-instances

I could write a whole book about WPT, but some smart people have already done so[24]. Additionally, the WPT forum[25] is a great place to share ideas and ask questions.

## PageSpeed Insights

PageSpeed Insights (introduced earlier in this chapter) offers an interface for running synthetic performance tests on a specific site. Following a test, you're presented with a result page like the one pictured:

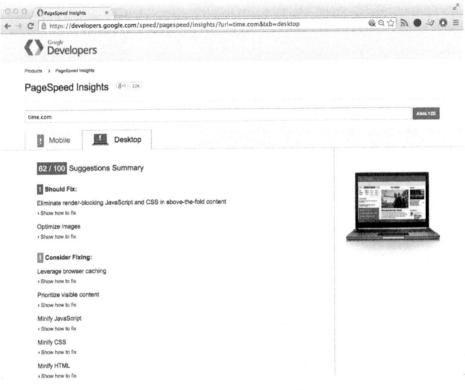

Figure 3.14. PageSpeed Insights data for time.com

PageSpeed Insights lacks some of the features of WPT, such as the advanced settings, the selection of test locations, a very detailed waterfall view, and a unique ID for each test. PageSpeed Insights only lets you type in the URL of the website. However, it automatically includes the test results for mobile users (something a WPT user

---

[24] http://shop.oreilly.com/product/0636920033592.do
[25] http://www.webpagetest.org/forums/

needs to choose explicitly). PageSpeed Insights also focuses more on optimization than WPT, offering helpful suggestions for optimizing your site.

## Browser Extensions and Plugins

There are various browser plugins and extensions offering additional ways to test your site's performance. Extensions like Firebug, YSlow, and PageSpeed Insights allow you to analyze your website on the spot via the browser.

Here is a quick summary of some of the tools available and their functionality:

- **Firebug**[26] helps you to inspect, log, profile, analyze and debug the page you are viewing in your browser. The **Net** tab is especially handy for analyzing perform-ance, as it presents all HTTP requests in a very detailed waterfall view.

- **YSlow**[27] can be installed as an add-on to the Firebug extension, but can also be added as a stand-alone plugin for most browsers. YSlow is the browser plugin answer to PageSpeed Insights and WPT. YSlow analyzes your web page according to Yahoo's rules for high performance websites[28]. It includes tools that not only help you diagnose but also triage on the spot.

- **PageSpeed Insights**[29] is available as plugin for Chrome and Firefox, providing suggestions on how to make your page faster. In addition, it rates the page based on several rules[30].

- **ShowSlow**[31] is an open-source website service as well as browser plugin that helps you monitor performance patterns. It combines the results of major per-formance tools including YSlow, Page Speed and WebPageTest.

## Advanced Analytical and Programming Tools

In addition to the tools above, there are some advanced analytical and programming tools you can use for synthetic measurement.

---

[26] http://getfirebug.com/

[27] https://developer.yahoo.com/yslow/

[28] https://developer.yahoo.com/performance/rules.html

[29] https://developers.google.com/speed/pagespeed/insights_extensions

[30] https://developers.google.com/speed/docs/insights/rules

[31] http://www.showslow.com/

## The Power to Query = Big Query + HTTP Archive

The current HTTP Archive SQL dump is around 400Gb of raw data. You probably don't want to download and import this into your database. How about using a tool that already has all the data imported, ready for you to query against? The answer is Big Query[32]. Big Query is a Google database tool that allows you to query big sets of databases via the browser. You can easily load the HTTP Archive project into your Big Query profile, and run any query you like against the HTTP Archive, while enjoying a blazing fast Google infrastructure.

This tool is very handy if you want to ask questions that haven't been answered by the HTTP Archive. For example, what are the most common third-party scripts? Check out BigQueri.es[33], a great community resource for finding answers to all sorts of performance questions.

## APIs

If you want to avoid manual monitoring and measuring, I'd suggest you take a look at some APIs on offer. With APIs, you can easily create helpful tools and integration checks. They can remove the need for manually opening the browser, going to WebPagetest or Page Speed, manually typing in the URL of the site you want to test, and so on. You can operate most of these tools via a command line interface (CLI).

**PageSpeed Insights API**

In order to use the PageSpeed Insights API, you'll need to acquire an API key[34].

The key is required for each API call you make. For example, you'd issue a cURL command like so:

```
curl GET "https://www.googleapis.com/page
➥speedonline/v1/runPagespeed?url=http://c
➥ode.google.com/speed/page-speed/&key={yo
➥urAPIKey}"
```

By default, the result comes back in JSON format:

---

[32] https://cloud.google.com/bigquery/what-is-bigquery

[33] http://bigqueri.es/

[34] https://developers.google.com/speed/docs/insights/v1/getting_started

```
{ "kind": "pagespeedonline#result",
➥"id": "http://time.com/",
➥"responseCode": 200,
...
➥"numberCssResources": 4 }
```

The JSON response[35], which I've only shown a nip-
pet of above, returns detailed information, such as
the size of each content type, the number of assets
per content type and the number of hosts contacted.
Can you spot which content type returns the highest
number of ResponseBytes? javascriptResponse-
Bytes represents the highest number of uncompressed response bytes for JavaScript resources on
the page, and returns 2535002 bytes, which is just
over 2.5Mb.

**WebPagetest API**

WebPagetest offers an API as well. It's up to you
which of the services you prefer.

After retrieving your API key from WebPagetest, you
can send a request as follows:

```
curl http://www.webpagetest.org/runtest.ph
➥p?f=json&url=www.time.com&k=<API KEY>
```

As I specified the format to be JSON (f=json), a
successful response will come back like this:

```
{ "statusCode":200, "statusText":"Ok",
➥ "data":{ "testId":"140907_R9_DQP",
...
➥"jsonUrl":"http:\/\/www.webpagetest.org
➥\/jsonResult.php?test=140907_R9_DQP",
...
```

The jsonUrl value includes the path to the actual
JSON WPT result:

---

[35] https://developers.google.com/speed/docs/insights/v1/reference

```
{ "data" : { "average" : { "firstView" : {
➥"TTFB" : 366, "adult_site" : 0, "aft" :
➥0, "avgRun" : 1, "bytesIn" : 1772202,
➥"bytesInDoc" : 1760651,
➥... "score_minify" : 100, ... }}}}}
```

This is just a snapshot and not the complete JSON response, but hopefully you get a sense of the valuable information stored in this response. As an example, any score_* value could be used for performance validation (if below 50, raise a flag, and so on).

There's a rate limit attached to the API key. This is another good reason to install your own WPT instance, as there'll be no rate limit then.

# Real User Monitoring

While synthetic testing focuses on one particular setup and doesn't show the "real" experience of a user, **real user monitoring** (RUM) tells you what an actual user is experiencing. It can't tell you how the user *feels* about the performance, but it will give you a good sense of how long it took them to view your page.

RUM can help you collect a lot of information about your users that synthetic testing can't, such as:

- **Cache**: RUM helps to better understand how much of your content is being cached by users.

- **Hardware**: RUM can reveal detailed information about the user's CPU, GPU and memory performance.

- **Browsers**: RUM can identify what kind of browsers load different pages.

- **Connectivity**: Internet connections can drop any moment (especially on mobile). RUM can help figure out where connections are slower.

Load times can vary a lot, based on several outside factors that you can't influence as a web developer. With RUM, you can get a better sense of what your actual users are experiencing in this regard. My own RUM experiences have revealed surprising data on how many people have lower or higher bandwidth than I originally expected.

So, how does RUM work? In order to perform real user monitoring, you need access to the user's browser data. There are two main APIs that help us collect and evaluate performance data coming right from our user's browser.

## Navigation Timing

The **Navigation Timing API**, introduced by the W3C Web Performance Working Group in 2012, allows developers to inquire about the page's performance via JavaScript. It's a great way to understand the end-to-end latency that your user experiences. The good news is that it's supported by most browsers.

The following graphic illustrates all the events that can be measured by JavaScript through the PerformanceTiming interface:

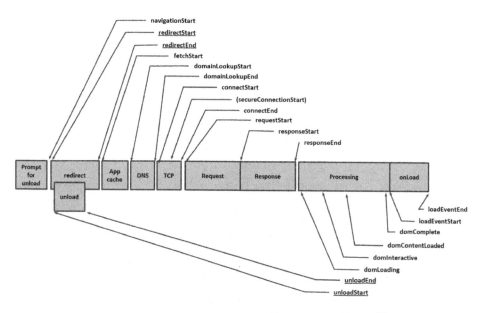

Figure 3.15. W3C processing model for the Navigation Timing API[36]

All of the above commands can be accessed via JavaScript to retrieve timing information for your page. Measuring the time of the events helps you assess the different phases of loading a page.

---

[36] http://www.w3.org/TR/navigation-timing/#processing-model

For example, imagine you want to retrieve the total page load time (PLT) via JavaScript. The following example does exactly that:

```
var page = performance.timing,
    plt = page.loadEventStart - page.navigationStart,

console.log(plt); // 34986, PLT output for specific user in ms;
```

Navigation timing only covers data concerning the entire page. So using this API might reveal that your page is slow, but what do you do then? To actually identify and diagnose performance issues with it, you need to look closer at each individual resource.

That's where the Resource Timing API comes in handy. It makes it possible to examine performance data for specific resources.

## Resource Timing

The **Resource Timing API** is a bit newer and not as well supported as the Navigation Timing API. With the Resource Timing API, you can dig deeper into understanding the behaviour of individual resources. Imagine you put an image on your page but you aren't sure how it performs in the real world. You want to know the TTFB data for this image.

As an example, let's pick the sitepoint.com logo[37]:

```
var img = window.performance.getEntriesByName("http://www.sitepoint.
➥com/wp-content/themes/sitepoint/assets/svg/sitepoint.svg")[0];
var ttfb = parseInt(img.responseStart - img.startTime),
total = parseInt(img.responseEnd - img.startTime);
console.log(ttfb); // output 85 (in ms)
console.log(total); // output 98 (in ms)

// you could now log this somewhere in a database
//or send an image beacon to your server
logPerformanceData('main logo', ttfb, total);
```

The logging would reveal how this image performs to users who viewed the image.

---

[37] http://www.sitepoint.com/wp-content/themes/sitepoint/assets/svg/sitepoint.svg

The following table shows the current browser support for the mentioned APIs:

| Browser | Navigation Timing API | Resource Timing API |
| --- | --- | --- |
| Chrome | ✔ | ✔ |
| Opera | ✔ | ✔ |
| IE >8 | ✔ | ✔ |
| Safari >7 | ✔ | |
| iOS Safari >7 | ✔ | |
| Firefox >30 | ✔ | |
| Android >4.3 | ✔ | ✔ |

*Browser support for Resource Timing API August 2014, source: caniuse.com*

## Free RUM Tools

### Boomerang

Boomerang[38] is an open source RUM tool that you are free to use under the GNU license.

Boomerang is based on the Navigation and Resource Timing APIs, collecting all information needed for assessing the performance and user experience of your site. For example, it can do anything that I've mentioned about the timing APIs above. You can examine such things as how long the DNS lookup took for a particular user, or what issues arose for a particular user demographic.

You can process and funnel RUM data into a beacon parsed by a script from your web server log files. This could then be put into a database or any other data storage. In Chapter 4, I'll show you how to analyze RUM data via boomerang.

### Google Analytics

Most performance measurements are recorded in median averages rather than mean. Google Analytics[39] (GA), however, is measured in mean. This approach might not seem too well suited to your goal, as it could also include outliers that skew your

---

[38] http://yahoo.github.io/boomerang/doc
[39] http://www.google.com/analytics/

results. In addition, Google's RUM sample rate is low, potentially not providing you with accurate real measurements.

However, if you already use GA and don't want to pay for a RUM service, or don't want to build your own RUM tracking tool, it's a great place to start.

> ### 💡 Mean, Median or 95th Percentile?
>
> **Arithmetic Mean (average):** take all values in your data set, and divide it by the total number of data points you summed up. Outliers are included in the calculation and this could result in skewing your data by pulling you away from the centre. Be aware that calculating outliers might change the entire meaning of your numbers and could cause false interpretations.
>
> **Median:** the most common measurement used in web performance. Line up each value in a selected data set in ascending order, and the single value in the middle of those values is your median. This approach gives you a more accurate representation of the load time of your website, seen by actual visitors.
>
> **95th percentile:** In order to measure performance, some also use the high percentiles like 80th, 90th or 95th percentile[40] instead of the median (50th percentile). For example, if the 95th percentile of a response time is 1000ms, that means that 5% of the collected data points are slower than 1000ms and 95% are faster than 1000ms.

### A/B Testing

For the purposes of RUM, you can use A/B testing to check if an enhancement you made to your website actually ends up enhancing your users' experience of the site. With some real data for both versions of the site, you can identify which is more successful and act accordingly.

## Comparing RUM and Synthetic

Now that you've learned about synthetic testing and RUM, you might wonder whether one technique is better than the other. It really depends on the question you want to answer.

---

[40] http://blog.catchpoint.com/2010/09/02/web_performance_metrics_best/

|  | **Synthetic** | **RUM** |
|---|---|---|
| **Who?** | You run the test | The user runs the test |
| **What?** | Measures the experience of one selected configuration (more like a lab environment) | Measures experience of "actual user" (casts a wide net, gives peace of mind), and you get to know your user better |
| **Why?** | Establishes a baseline performance level | Get concrete information about users' latency, bandwidth, page load time, etc. |
| **How?** | Tools: private/public WebPagetest (API), PageSpeed Insights (API), and commercial products | Tools: Boomerang.js, Google Analytics, and commercial products |

Having a combination of synthetic and real user data will help you cover your entire measurement spectrum.

Several analogies have been made to compare the approaches of RUM and synthetic measurement. One that I really like is the following: RUM is the floodlight and synthetic is the flashlight[41]. With synthetic testing, the flashlight, you focus on one specific thing. Anything outside of that, you won't see. The floodlight, corresponding to RUM, reveals all kinds of different findings.

# Cool Down

Let's review some of the takeaways from this chapter:

- Measurement data is essential for tracking progress.

- Don't always go by one unit only. Just because a website has a lot of images doesn't mean it's slower than a page that has no images.

- A waterfall is a great tool for identifying performance bottlenecks.

---

[41] https://blogs.akamai.com/2012/12/situational-performance-measurement-with-a-splash-of-rum.html

- HTTP Archive and WebPagetest are important performance tools for measuring website performance.

- PageSpeed and Speed Index capture the overall performance of a page.

- If you love to code and interact with APIs, it's worth incorporating your performance budget into your continuous deployment process. It will remove a lot of manual work.

- Synthetic testing and RUM are useful processes that work well together.

Congratulations, you've learned a lot in this chapter. We'll now proceed to put it all into practice as we start our boot camp.

# Performance Boot Camp Setup

## Warm Up

So far in this book, we've identified the fundamental issues of web performance and how to measure them. In this and the following chapters, we'll begin to take steps to address these performance issues.

Our aim is to create lean websites, and for that we need to establish an exercise routine, so to speak—a set of procedures to ensure that our sites are fast, responsive and enjoyable for our users.

Just as we might sign up for an intensive boot camp course to make our bodies lean, so let's get started on our web performance boot camp. To prepare ourselves, we'll take the following steps:

- set up a monitoring mechanism for recording the performance of our website in order to understand what to optimize for

- establish a performance budget as a goal to focus on.

# Measure First, *Then* Optimize Towards a Goal

Before setting any goals, you first need to audit the performance of your website. Run your site through WebPagetest (WPT) if you haven't already done so. While you have a wide range of performance tools at your disposal (as we saw in Chapter 3), I'll mostly be using WPT and the browser's developer tools for the upcoming examples.

## Your Website's Waterfall

After you run WPT or load the network panel in your browser's developer tools, you'll have detailed access to the website's waterfall. The next step is to spot any potential performance problems in the waterfall.

Let's pick an example waterfall and analyze its formation. Check out the waterfall in Figure 4.1: it's an analysis of a sample page that I created and will be using throughout the next few chapters. It includes several individual JavaScript and CSS files, and some images of dogs:

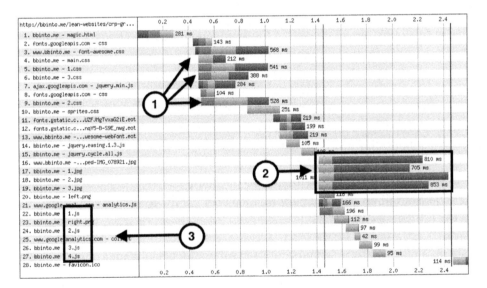

Figure 4.1. *Waterfall view for sample page*[1]

---

[1] http://bbinto.me/lean-websites/crp-grunt/without/magic.html

Let's note three things about the waterfall results pictured above:

1. Line items 3,5,9 show big bodies of CSS assets. Loading too many different and large CSS files after one another will delay the rendering of the page, and specifically slow down the Start Render time.

2. Several image assets are being requested in line items 16–19, and they all consist of relatively big bodies. It's best to aim for a "thin" waterfall, as this correlates to small resources (or small file sizes). Each asset or request should load quickly, that means the body of the asset should be small.

3. Numerous small JavaScript files are being requested in line items 22, 24, 26 and 27. The fewer requests you make, the smaller and "steeper" the waterfall will be. A steep waterfall is a great indicator of a lean website, revealing proper sharing and parallelizing of resources.

### Resource Not Found

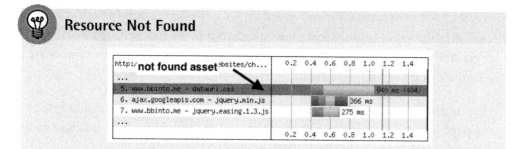

Figure 4.2. An asset was not found

Avoid red lines in your WPT waterfall, as shown in Figure 4.2. These indicate that the resource could not be found. The cause for this could be that the asset is not referenced properly in the markup (the wrong path is given, for example), or the asset doesn't exist on the server. Please note that the WPT waterfall marks "not found" assets as red, whereas many other waterfall visualizers—such as your browser's **Network** tab—will not highlight them. Performance will suffer from a "not found" asset in the waterfall, because the browser is wasting precious time trying to locate the file while still having to parse the rest of the page.

Throughout the next few chapters, we'll discuss how to optimize and fix the issues we've just discovered, whilst monitoring the improvement of the page's performance.

# Performance Monitoring: Set up Your Performance Dashboard

It's important that you frequently monitor your website's performance, as it can easily be degraded by such things as third party scripts or bloated images. A **performance monitoring dashboard** is handy for keeping track of your site's performance, and will provide you with peace of mind as well.

Here are tools and processes that I propose you could consider:

- Set up a private instance of HTTP Archive to track trends, over time, for a defined list of domains. This will help you measure current issues and also anticipate improvements in the future. By auditing trends, you can specifically tackle newly introduced performance issues that you wouldn't have noticed otherwise.

- Calibrate your synthetic measurements with some real user results, by creating a RUM solution to capture and understand your real users' settings. This can be very helpful in finding out about specific latency bottlenecks, for example, or bandwidth issues of your users.

- Create alerts to notify you if your website goes above a certain threshold (such as page load time, or server response time). You can rely on both free and commercial products to help you with that.

## Create Your Private HTTP Archive

The public HTTP Archive collects web trends of the Top Alexa websites[2], and if you're lucky, your website is one of them and is being captured. (If not, you can add[3] your website to the list.)

If your site isn't listed, however, or isn't (yet) accessible via the Internet, then it won't be possible to monitor and track trends via the public HTTP Archive.

Thankfully, as noted earlier, HTTP Archive is an open-source project that can be cloned for your own use. For example, if your company has many subdomains, internal websites, or different micro sites that you want to track, installing your own

---

[2] http://httparchive.org/about.php#listofurls
[3] http://httparchive.org/addsite.php

HTTP Archive instance will be very beneficial. You could even add your competitors' websites to compare their pages with yours. All of the data will be stored in a local database, organized into several data tables of requests, pages, the list of URLs to check, and more. Hence, you can run ad hoc SQL queries against the data to gather all kinds of useful information.

In order to set up HTTP Archive, you need a web server with MySQL and PHP. You'll also need to request an API key so that the HTTP Archive instance can execute runs on the public WPT. (If you choose to run your own private instance of WebPagetest instead—in order to skip waiting times when being in a queue to run your test from the public instance—you don't have to use an API key.) If you need step-by-step instructions on how to setup your own HTTP Archive data set and database, please check out my blog post "Set up your own HTTP Archive to track and query your site trends[4]".

Once you have your private HTTP Archive database set up and filled with data, you can then run queries based on it. In order to provide you with some "real" results, I decided to use the HTTP Archive instance from one of my previous projects.

Let's start with a couple of questions that can be answered via the captured data. Please note that the following examples use SQL to query the database. If you aren't familiar with SQL queries, check out some courses[5] or tutorials[6], and review some of the HTTP Archive queries[7] by Ilya Grigorik to get you started.

## How Big Is the Biggest Image?

Run the following query to reveal the answer to this question:

```
SELECT req.url, req.respSize, req.mimeType, pages.url FROM requests
➥ as req
JOIN (SELECT url , pageid, rank FROM pages) as pages
```

---

[4] http://www.bbinto.me/performance/setup-your-own-http-archive-to-track-and-query-your-site-trends/

[5] https://www.coursera.org/course/db

[6] https://www.udacity.com/course/viewer#!/c-cs253/l-48756013/m-48691560

[7] https://gist.github.com/igrigorik/5801492

```
ON pages.pageid = req.pageid
WHERE req.mimeType like 'image%'
ORDER by req.respSize DESC
```

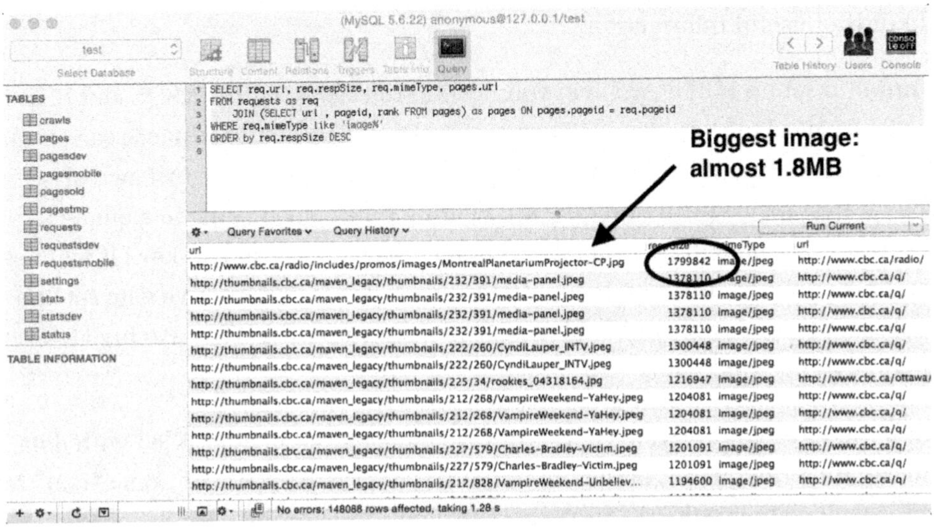

Figure 4.3. Discovering the biggest image used

## What Is the Slowest Page?

You can discover the slowest page by running the following query, shown in Figure 4.4:

```
SELECT url, renderStart
FROM pages
GROUP BY url
ORDER BY renderStart DESC
```

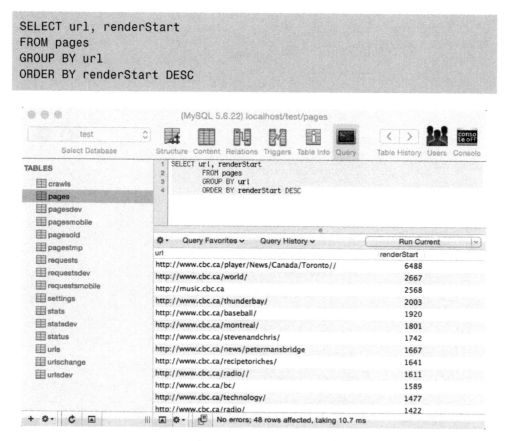

Figure 4.4. Analyzing render start times

## What Pages Exceed 200 Requests Per Page?

Let's find pages that are making more than 200 requests, shown in Figure 4.5:

```
SELECT url, reqTotal
FROM pages WHERE reqTotal > 200
GROUP BY url
ORDER BY reqTotal DESC
```

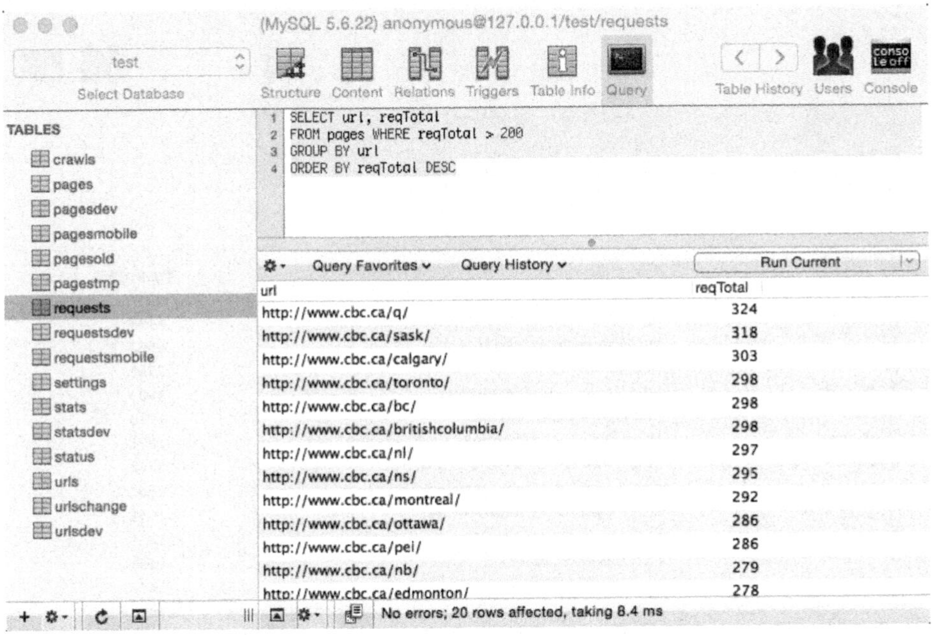

Figure 4.5. Finding pages that exceed 200 requests

Going through the results table of this query will help you identify bottlenecks and verify if the page really needs to fetch more than 200 assets.

## Create Your Private RUM Tests

boomerang.js[8] is an open-source tool that can help you track RUM data. The following section will outline, in a few simple steps, how you can set up RUM for your site.

---

[8] http://yahoo.github.io/boomerang/doc/

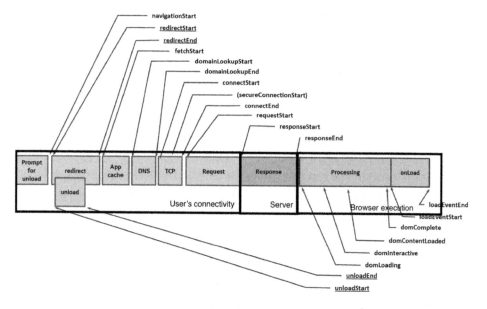

Figure 4.6. How the Navigation Timing API is structured[9]

As a refresher, the Navigation Timing API provides access to different events throughout the journey of a page being delivered to the user. There are the user's connectivity events, the server events, as well as the events executed by the browser (from left to right in Figure 4.6). For example, we can go ahead and measure the server response time:

```
var page = performance.timing,
rt = page.responseEnd - page.responseStart,

console.log(rt); // server response time
```

In order to track any information about your users, JavaScript code needs to be included in the page that is to be tested.

You can track your users' performance data by creating a **beacon** that will send the RUM results back to your server. A beacon is a request made purely to send performance data back to your server. Until the W3C Beacon API[10] is available, you'll need to create a beacon yourself. The value is in the request itself, and the response is actually not important; but to make initiating the request easier, it's normally con-

---

[9] https://www.igvita.com/slides/2012/html5devconf/#8
[10] http://www.w3.org/TR/beacon/

venient to request a tiny image (such as **beacon.gif**), including several parameters, and be logged on your web server.

Let's try this out ourselves. I will show you how to track RUM data on my personal website.

1. First, place the boomerang script into your page. Ideally, place it at the bottom, to avoid obstructing any essential page assets.

   The script below shows you how I use the beacon to send performance data. I created a transparent 1x1px GIF, uploaded it to the web server, and set the beacon_url path to its location:

```
<script src="http://bbinto.me/lean-websites/chapter-4/rum/
➥boomerang/boomerang.custom.min.js" type="text/javascript">
➥</script>
<script type="text/javascript">
    BOOMR.init({
        beacon_url: "http://bbinto.me/lean-websites/chapter-4/rum
➥/boomerang/images/beacon.gif"
        });
</script>
```

2. Once the script has been included, reload the page. In the browser's console, you'll be able to see what kind of data boomerang has started to collect:

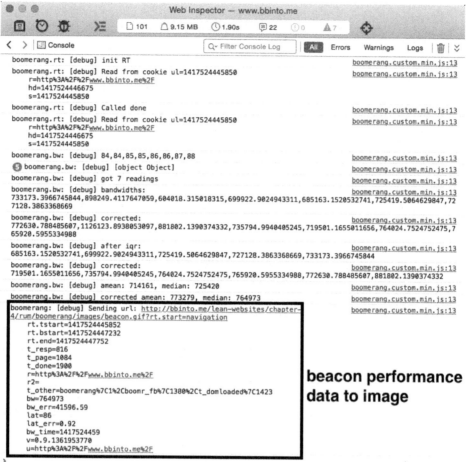

Figure 4.7. Checking out boomerang data in the console

3. A simple log parser can now scan through the logs to extract the data. Check out the log file entry below as an example. `beacon.gif` lists the same boomerang data that we saw in the console above:

```
99.231.246.80 - - [02/Dec/2014:05:47:38 -0700]
"GET /lean-websites/chapter-4/rum/boomerang/images/beacon.gif?
rt.start=navigation&
rt.tstart=1417524445852&
rt.bstart=1417524447232&
rt.end=1417524447752&
t_resp=816&
```

```
t_page=1084&
t_done=1900&
r=http%3A%2F%2Fwww.bbinto.me%2F&
r2=&
t_other=boomerang%7C1%2Cboomr_fb%7C1380%2Ct_domloaded%7C1423&
bw=764973&
bw_err=41596.59&
lat=86&
lat_err=0.92&
bw_time=1417524459&
v=0.9.1361953770&
u=http%3A%2F%2Fwww.bbinto.me%2F HTTP/1.1" 200 35
➥ "http://www.bbinto.me/" "Mozilla/5.0 (Macintosh; Intel Mac OS
➥ X 10_10_1)
```

From the data above, we can draw the following conclusions about my visit to bbinto.me:

- t_done: my perceived load time of the page was 1084ms

- bw: my measured bandwidth was 764973 bytes per second (or 747KB/s)

- lat: my measured HTTP latency was 86ms (or 0.08 seconds).

For more information about the remaining parameters, please check out the boomerang page[11].

4. Now that I have extracted the data from the log file, I can export the result to a spreadsheet or into a database to query it, and use it to create charts for better illustration. I decided to save it as a CSV spreadsheet that can be opened in Excel. The screenshot below highlights the same set of data that was triggered as soon as I refreshed the page in step 2.

5. I kept the beacon in place on the site for two days to gather real user data, and by the end I had approximately 300 data points—real visits from real users that I could analyze:

---

[11] http://yahoo.github.io/boomerang/doc/howtos/howto-0.html

| Date | bw | lat | t_done | UA |
|---|---|---|---|---|
| 02/Dec/2014:05:38:16 -0700 | 550207 | 105 | 2336 | Mozilla/5.0 (Macintosh; Intel Mac OS X 10_10_1) AppleWebKit/537.36 (KHTML, like Gecko) Chrome/38.0.2125.122 Safari/537.36 |
| 02/Dec/2014:05:40:19 -0700 | 919341 | 97 | 6014 | Mozilla/5.0 (Macintosh; Intel |
| 02/Dec/2014:05:42:32 -0700 | 871323 | 85 | 2435 | Mozilla/5.0 (Macint... RUM data via beacon |
| 02/Dec/2014:05:46:23 -0700 | 644275 | 88 | 3655 | Mozilla/5.0... intosh; Intel Mac OS X 10_10_1) AppleWebKit/600.1.25 (KHTML, like Gecko) Version/8.0 Safari/600.1.25 |
| 02/Dec/2014:05:47:38 -0700 | 764973 | 86 | 1900 | Mozilla/5.0 (Macintosh; Intel Mac OS X 10_10_1) AppleWebKit/600.1.25 (KHTML, like Gecko) Version/8.0 Safari/600.1.25 |
| 02/Dec/2014:05:48:26 -0700 | 550207 | 105 | 3784 | Mozilla/5.0 (Macintosh; Intel Mac OS X 10_10_1) AppleWebKit/537.36 (KHTML, like Gecko) Chrome/38.0.2125.122 Safari/537.36 |
| 02/Dec/2014:06:25:14 -0700 | 550207 | 105 | 3508 | Mozilla/5.0 (Macintosh; Intel Mac OS X 10_10_1) AppleWebKit/537.36 (KHTML, like Gecko) Chrome/38.0.2125.122 Safari/537.36 |
| 02/Dec/2014:08:13:29 -0700 | 1550795 | 280 | 0 | Mozilla/5.0 (iPhone; CPU iPhone OS 7_1_2 like Mac OS X) AppleWebKit/537.51.2 (KHTML, like Gecko) Mobile/11D257 |
| 02/Dec/2014:08:28:26 -0700 | 0 | 0 | 48767 | Mozilla/5.0 (Macintosh; Intel Mac OS X 10_10_0) AppleWebKit/537.36 (KHTML, like Gecko) Chrome/39.0.2171.71 Safari/537.36 |

Figure 4.8. A snippet of RUM data collected from beacon, via log files, exported as CSV and stored in a spreadsheet

The screenshot shown in Figure 4.8 displays what I recorded: the exact time the user accessed the page (`Date`), bandwidth (`bw`), latency (`lat`), page load time (`t_done`), and the corresponding user agent (`UA`). Additionally, with the help of simple spreadsheet functions, I determined the distribution of RUM load times, user latency and bandwidth.

The following three metrics are useful in understanding your users' experiences when visiting your site:

■ **Page load time**: the following graph describes the distribution of load times in milliseconds for bbinto.me, retrieved from all `t_done` data points. You can see that most users experience a page load time between 3 and 5 seconds. The page loads in under 5 seconds for half of the visitors. 95% of visitors experienced a load time of below 19.1 seconds:

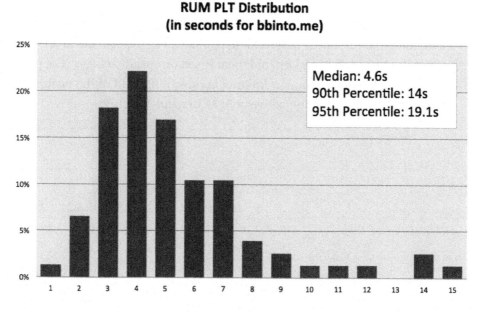

Figure 4.9. Page load time distribution

■ **Latency**: latency was recorded by collecting `lat` values from the beacon. Half of the visits have to deal with a latency around 166ms. 95% of visitors had a latency of under 370ms (95th percentile):

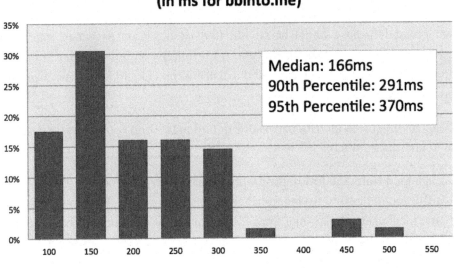

Figure 4.10. Latency distribution

■ **Bandwidth**: another interesting RUM experiment is to look at the bandwidth, listed under bw. As shown in the example below, I aggregated all data points for bw from the spreadsheet and filtered them based on specific ranges. The pie chart below shows the most common Internet connections. Half of the visitors came to my site with a connection between 512KB/s and 1.6MB/s:

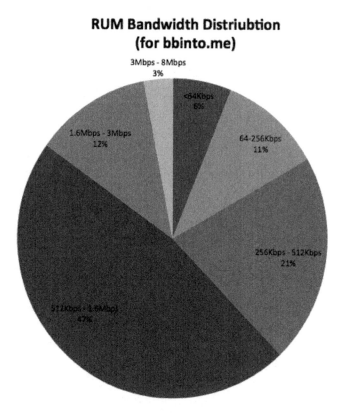

Figure 4.11. Bandwidth distribution

 **Boomerang's Methodology**

Page load time is computed by first recording the time of the `onbeforeunload` event, which is then stored in a cookie. This is followed by recording the time of the `onload` event and subtracting that from the stored time in the cookie. Subsequently, latency and bandwidth are measured by downloading fixed size images from a server and measuring the time it took to download them. You can refer to more details of methodology[12] on the boomerang website.

By looking at these results, you'll notice that I'm closer to understanding my actual, real users. For example, knowing their average connection speed will help me decide if my audience arrives at my site via high-speed connection or lower-speed connec-

---

[12] http://yahoo.github.io/boomerang/doc/methodology.html

tions. I can then cater for that specific scenario—perhaps by serving fewer or smaller images, or avoiding specific assets altogether.

 **Help with Getting Boomerang Set Up**

If you need additional help with setting up RUM, I suggest that you read up on the boomerang how-to docs[13] or use Captain Rum[14], a simple script that I created.

Rather than creating your own beacon solution, you could use the Beacon API[15], introduced by the World Wide Web Consortium (W3C)—though it's currently in working draft, and not supported by IE or Safari as yet. Its intent is to make it easier for web developers to send analytics or diagnostic information back to the server.

**RUM and High-traffic Sites**

If your website receives a lot of traffic, you'll encounter a huge amount of beacon data in your log files. Hence, parsing the log files and extracting the data can be slow. Consider introducing some code to use a lower sample rate, or just enable the code during specific times of the day.

# Set Up Alerts

Monitoring your site with automated alerts—which notify you if something unwanted happens to your website—is a useful technique for avoiding surprises. There are several commercial products available, as well as free tools.

Here are some examples of basic alerts you can set up for your website:

- Get notified if your website is not available to your visitors.

- Get notified if any issues occur based on geographic or platform-specific events.

- Get notified if performance measurements reach a specific threshold, such as page load times exceeding 10 seconds, or server response times exceeding two seconds.

---

[13] http://www.lognormal.com/boomerang/doc/howtos/
[14] https://github.com/bbinto/captain-rum
[15] http://www.w3.org/TR/beacon/

## Google Analytics

If you already use Google Analytics, you may as well leverage its free custom alerts. While I mentioned that Analytics only uses sampled data, and relies on the average measurements instead of the median to calculate performance metrics, it is still a quick and easy alert tool. Go to **Admin -> Custom Alerts** to create your custom alert[16], as shown in Figure 4.12:

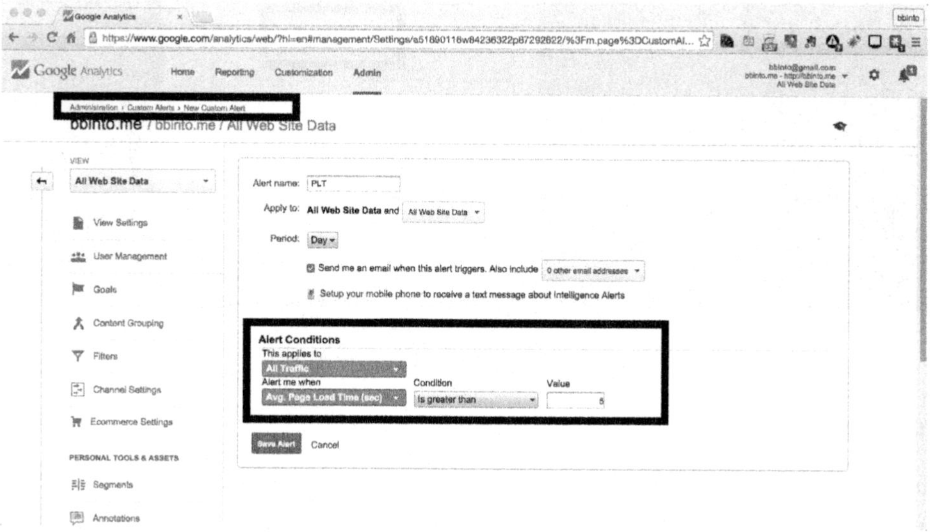

Figure 4.12. Setting an alert in Google Analytics

## Pingdom

Though Pingdom is a commercial monitoring tool, it's also available in a free limited version[17]. The free version might be enough if you only want RUM reporting and alerts of website downtime. A great feature of Pingdom is that it allows you to choose between "average" or "median" measurement.

The following Figure 4.13 screenshot shows how to set up alerts to notify you when your website is down:

---

[16] https://www.igvita.com/2012/11/30/web-performance-anomaly-detection-with-google-analytics/
[17] https://www.pingdom.com/free/

Figure 4.13. Setting a downtime alert in Pingdom

## CopperEgg

CopperEgg[18] is one of many commercial tools that provides flexibility in setting up alerts, RUM, and other measurements. The Figure 4.14 screenshot below shows an example of how granular you can get when setting up alerts for specific performance metrics. It's a handy suite of monitoring tools that will give you peace of mind.

---

[18] http://copperegg.com/

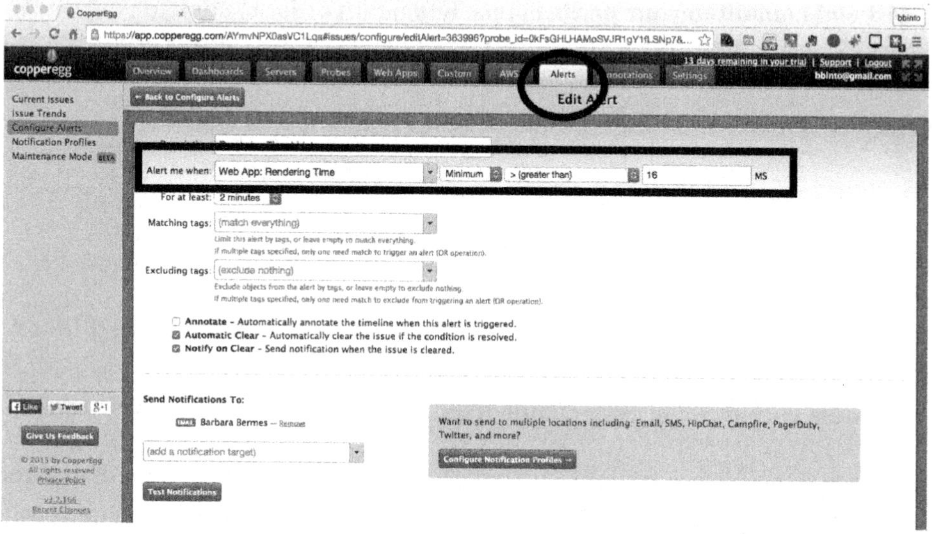

Figure 4.14. Setting an alert in CopperEgg

# Set up a Performance Budget

By setting a **performance budget**, you can ensure that a defined baseline in values for various performance metrics should not be exceeded. For example, this could mean setting target values for page size or the amount of HTTP requests used on a page.

Finding a budget that is realistic, measurable, and achievable is a great start for a leaner website. It provides goals that the whole team can focus on, and will help you answer questions like "What are we trying to improve?" and "What will the measurement for success be?"

But where to start? How do you set up a budget for your website?

Here are some pointers to help you set a budget and stick to it:

- **Assess the standards of your competitors**: your competitors' metrics can help you establish a performance baseline.

- **Create performance hypotheses to strengthen business metrics**: come up with assumptions on how to make your website more successful by making it faster.

■ **List and commit to your performance budget**: in order to stick to your budget, you need to publish it, and commit to your performance metrics and thresholds.

Let's take a look at each of these in more detail.

# Competitive Comparison

"The wise learn many things from their enemies." — Aristophanes

Once you have your current site performance data, it can sometimes be difficult to determine which results should be improved. One idea is to compare your performance results with those of your competitors.

WPT is a great resource for running competitive analysis. Click the **Visual Comparison** tab when you first land on the WPT website. It lets you add several different websites for comparison. Comparing your site with a competitor's can give you a useful and tangible baseline for your website's performance.

For example, let's assume you have a clothing retail website. You'd probably want to make sure that users could browse your landing page faster than a competing clothing retail site. That's where you can apply the WPT "Visual Comparison" tool.

For now, let's call your site Website A, and the competitor's site Website B.

1. Go to WPT and click the **Visual Comparison** tab. Type in your website and your competitor's website to retrieve the comparative performance data and filmstrips, as shown in Figure 4.15.

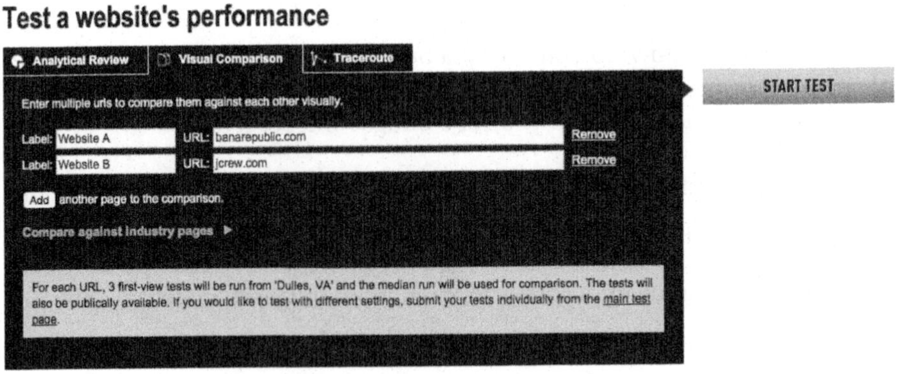

Figure 4.15. Starting a visual comparison on WPT

2. Once the comparison test is completed, you'll be presented with filmstrips of Websites A and B, as shown in Figure 4.16. The first visible content is delivered immediately by Website B, whereas Website A is only starting to show useful content above the fold after 6 seconds.

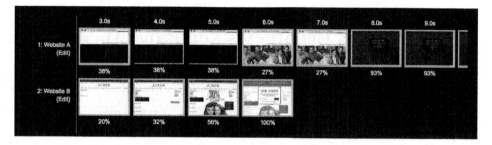

Figure 4.16. WPT filmstrips comparing two clothing store websites

3. Here are some additional measurements:

| Competitive Performance Comparison | Website A[19] | Website B[20] |
|---|---|---|
| SpeedIndex | 6197 | 4483 |
| Bytes (Fully Loaded) | 4,761KB | 1,915KB |
| Visually Complete | 9.300s | 5.700s |

There's definitely room for improvement for website A, as it's clearly not performing as well as website B. Each category above shows huge differences between the two. Website A comes out with more than double the total page size of Website B.

Try this out yourself: consider who is your biggest competitor, what website is similar to yours, or what website do you admire when it comes to speed. Measure against it, and set your budget.

[20] http://www.webpagetest.org/result/141211_NV_NN5/1/details/

[19] http://www.webpagetest.org/result/141211_NJ_NN6/3/details/

> **Alternative to WPT**
>
> Besides using WPT's visual comparison, you can also use SpeedCurve[21], a visually pleasing, cloud-based tool that lets you benchmark sites against competitors and industry categories.

# Create Business Hypotheses and Prove Them

Spend some time understanding how site speed could dictate your business metrics and vice versa. If you need buy-in from management to speed up your site, the best way to do so is by aligning your performance goals with real business data. Can negative performance results directly correlate with bad business performance?

It's important to figure out if there's a correlation between these two phenomena. You might require the help of a product manager, or a marketing/sales team to investigate user behaviours on the site. Ask them for data that will provide you with the biggest "pain" points for your current website. Look for clues suggesting that performance is your conversion bottleneck.

The goal is to come up with hypotheses related to performance that can be validated with concrete data and then be improved upon.

Let's talk through a simple example. Imagine you maintain an ecommerce website selling furniture, and you've conducted performance analyses of your competitors and defined your #1 competitor. You want to make sure people will purchase furniture through your website instead of your competitor's. Now, let's create some hypotheses and goals. A good start is to compare what elements are loaded first on your website vs. the competitor's website. For example, check if your "call to action" (CTA)[22] buttons load faster than those on the competitor's site. Or compare what content is visible above the fold.

Here are some sample observations that might help in forming hypotheses for a furniture ecommerce website:

---

[21] http://speedcurve.com
[22] CTA buttons could be "Buy", "Shop" and so on, depending on what you want your visitor to achieve with their visit.

| Observation | Hypothesis |
|---|---|
| "Winter sales were very low this year, and nobody clicked on our special discount button" | By ensuring that the special discount button is more prominent and loads as quickly as possible, we'll increase sales and market share (to compete with the competitor) |
| "Fewer visitors to the site than two months ago" | By removing or optimizing an asset—such as a heavy hero image—we'll increase our visitor numbers |
| "Visitors drop off during the checkout process" | By improving the page load time of the checkout process, the drop off rate will reduce |

Based on these observations, the table above shows how you can put on your performance hat, make assumptions, and then come up with specific budget goals.

You could further use A/B testing, as described in Chapter 3, to test out different options in order to collect data that shows what changes will have the biggest impact.

The hypotheses above are valid assumptions, and have worked for retail and shopping sites in the past. For example, boosting AutoAnything.com[23]'s page load time improved sales by 13%. Another real-world example[24] comes from Mozilla: cutting their page load time by 2 seconds resulted in a 15.4% increase in downloads. The sooner you get your content to users, the sooner they can interact with it, and the more you benefit.

Can you think of potential performance bottlenecks for your website that could negatively influence the business?

## List and Commit to Your Performance Metrics

Once you've gathered enough baseline data and created a competitive performance analysis, it's time to turn them into official goals, and commit to them.

---

[23] http://www.radware.com/PleaseRegister.aspx?returnUrl=6442452828
[24] https://blog.mozilla.org/metrics/2010/04/05/firefox-page-load-speed-%E2%80%93-part-ii/

1. List your current performance data. I'll continue to use the sample page I introduced at the beginning of the chapter as an example. The following data was taken from the WPT results[25] for the page:

| WPT Metrics | Results |
| --- | --- |
| Fully Loaded | 2.58s |
| SpeedIndex | 2222 |
| Bytes (Fully Loaded) | 692KB |

2. Prioritize results that could be improved. I propose starting with the most obvious results—the low-hanging fruit. For example, you could tackle the "Fully Loaded" result first, aiming to reduce it to under 2 seconds—nearly a 30% decrease in page load time.

Be ambitious, but also stay realistic, making sure these goals are achievable. There's always room for further improvement. Start with your first goal of 2 seconds, then measure performance and business data again to assess the effectiveness your approach.

| Priority | Metric | WPT Results | Budget Goal |
| --- | --- | --- | --- |
| 1 | Fully Loaded | 2.58s | =< 2s |
| 3 | Bytes (Fully Loaded) | 692KB | *will automatically improve after goal #1 is achieved* |
| 2 | SpeedIndex | 2222 | *will automatically improve after goal #1 is achieved* |

In addition, if you gather RUM data for your website, as I did it for bbinto.me earlier, you can also specify a target for the RUM page load time, to ensure that your real users "really" benefit from the changes. bbinto.me showed a median of 4.6s for RUM PLT. For this example, we could aim for 3 seconds.

---

[25] http://www.webpagetest.org/result/150123_B7_2RD/

3. Commit to your goals. Don't just talk about them; circulate and publish them amongst the team so everybody is reminded—even print them out and hang them up somewhere if that helps. Etsy does a great job in publicly exposing the performance of their website. They publish their performance results[26] quarterly. It's their way of committing to performance, and it's a great idea.

---

### What Speed Index and PageSpeed Score Should You Aim For?

- Aim for a *low* Speed Index. As Paul Irish defines it, a site with a Speed Index under 10000 is considered fast[27].

- Aim for a *high* PageSpeed value. Google considers websites scored with 85 to be performing well[28].

---

In the following chapters, I'll show you how to turn these goals into actual results and success.

# Cool Down

- You've learned how to spot performance problems in a waterfall: aim for short and steep waterfalls.

- You've learned how to setup your own performance dashboard, starting with a private HTTP Archive instance, and collecting RUM data to understand your users' bandwidth, load times, and more importantly latency. In addition, you've been introduced to monitoring products and alert systems to help you combat performance.

- You've learned how to set realistic performance goals based on the RUM measurements of your site, WPT results, as well as competitive comparison analysis.

- Overall, you've been guided to spot performance problems for your own website. Now let's fix them!

---

[26] https://codeascraft.com/2014/08/01/q2-2014-site-performance-report/
[27] http://timkadlec.com/2014/01/fast-enough/#comment-1200946500
[28] https://developers.google.com/speed/docs/insights/about

# Mastering Lean HTTP Requests

## Warm Up

We've learned that latency is one of the biggest bottlenecks when it comes to web performance. The best way to reduce latency is to cut down the amount of HTTP requests the browser has to make, and to minimize the size of each individual asset being requested. In order to understand how to master lean HTTP requests, I will first explain how the browser processes them. After helping you grasp how the browser works, I'll discuss several ways to scale down and optimize HTTP requests, such as image spriting, concatenation, and minification.

## Understanding How the Browser Works

By understanding how the browser renders your content, you'll gain a lot of insight into how to structure and order your page elements. The browser has the task of loading assets, called HTTP requests. As we've seen from dissecting an HTTP transaction, each asset has several metrics attached to it to help measure its performance.

The following process diagram shows what steps the browser goes through to render a page and its assets. **Rendering**—the process of displaying the requested content in the browser window—is the primary function of a browser:

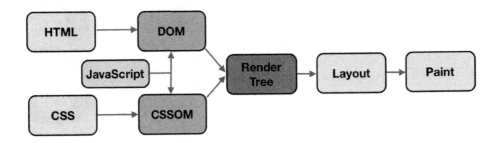

Figure 5.1. How the browser renders

### The Rendering Rule

Any ambiguity that the browser encounters when rendering a page will block rendering until it's resolved. Make sure to provide your browser with clean markup and instructions on how to render your page.

Let's go through the diagram shown in Figure 5.1:

**HTML**

HTML parsing is a crucial piece in the rendering puzzle and leads to the construction of the document object model. Parsing happens incrementally, so that the browser can discover required and upcoming requests while sending the necessary responses.

**Document Object Model**

The browser parses the HTML document to construct a **document object model** (DOM)—a tree structure that describes the elements on the page.

**CSS**

The CSS is **render blocking**, which means that the browser needs to load *all* CSS files referenced in the HTML markup prior to rendering the content. Without styling, a page can be impractical and sometimes even unusable. An effect called the "**flash of unstyled content**" (FOUC) could happen if your CSS is loaded too far towards the bottom of the page.

**CSS Object Model**

In addition to parsing the HTML, the browser also has to process the style sheets (the CSS) in order to understand how the elements in the DOM should be displayed. We refer to this as the CSS Object Model (CSSOM). Both the DOM and the CSSOM together allow the browser to paint the page.

**JavaScript**

JavaScript adds the power to manipulate and interact with the DOM, causing the render tree to change. If that happens, rendering is blocked until the browser has parsed and executed the script. JavaScript can be loaded synchronously, blocking the DOM, or asynchronously, which will not interrupt document parsing. JavaScript won't run until the CSSOM is fully loaded.

Different browsers run on different JavaScript engines. Depending on your users' browsers, they might experience the performance of your website differently, especially if it's a heavy JavaScript web application.

**Render Tree**

The **render tree** combines the content and style information of the entire visible content on the screen. It is the event where the DOM and CSSOM come together.

Not all nodes from the DOM will end up in the render tree. For example, scripts and meta tags are non-visible elements and won't be seen by the user.

In addition, the `visibility: hidden` style declaration won't insert its child(ren) into the render tree, but it will be rendered and displayed as an empty box. Elements (nodes) using the `display:none` style declaration, however, won't be added to the render tree.

**Layout**

While the render tree gets us closer to actually seeing content on the screen, there is still something important missing: this process doesn't define the position or size of each node on the page. That is what the **layout** step takes care of.

**Paint**

The final step is to **paint** the pixels. The style sheets define how expensive the paint process will be. If you have complicated styles, such as drop shadows or CSS animations, this could add complexity to your render tree, resulting in a slower load time. The paint step will reveal if your website, when scrolled, is jank-free or not. Repainting is expensive for the graphics processing unit (GPU) and can cause your page to feel clunky when scrolling.

 **Jank**

**Jank** refers to anything that feels clunky or delayed when scrolling through a page. It's basically the opposite of smooth scrolling. For example, jank effects can occur when JavaScript tries to repaint a lot of content during an `onscroll` handler.

 **JavaScript Engines**

Some popular engines are Nitro, SpiderMonkey, V8 and Chakra:

| Engine | Browser |
|---|---|
| Nitro (JavaScriptCore) | Safari |
| SpiderMonkey | Firefox |
| V8 | Google Chrome |
| Chakra | Internet Explorer |

Douglas Crockford, the "father of JavaScript", built a representative performance benchmark tool to compare JavaScript engines:

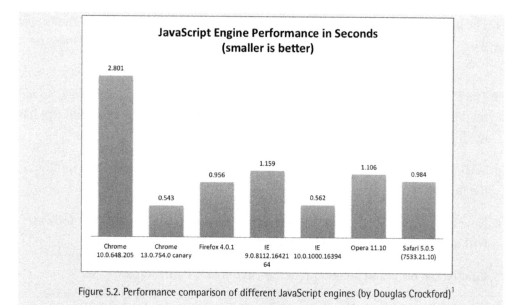

Figure 5.2. Performance comparison of different JavaScript engines (by Douglas Crockford)[1]

# Critical Rendering Path

By going through the page rendering process above, we have actually traversed through what's known as the **critical rendering path** (CRP). The CRP describes the code and resources that are required to render the initial view of a page—or the visible, above the fold part.

Let's traverse through the CRP with a basic example:

```
1.  <html>
2.    <head>
3.       <link rel="stylesheet" href="style.css">
4.    </head>
5.    <body>
6.       <div>Hello Friends!</div>
7.       <img src="bbinto.jpg">
8.       <script src="load_map.js"></script>
9.    </body>
10. </html>
```

There are several steps that happen to render this page:

---

[1] http://javascript.crockford.com/performance.html

1. The browser begins to construct the DOM after it receives the HTML. That's also when the browser discovers the `link` tag and sends the request to retrieve the CSS.

2. The CSSOM can only be built when CSS has arrived, which is why the CSS is render blocking. The DOM building can't be finished yet, because JavaScript has not been parsed.

3. Once the CSS arrives, the browser can build the CSSOM, which then unblocks the JavaScript.

4. Now the JavaScript can load, which unblocks the DOM to finish. The browser will merge DOM and CSSOM into the Render Tree.

5. Finally, the browser can complete the Layout and Paint steps.

Figure 5.3 illustrates what's happening as the browser completes these steps:

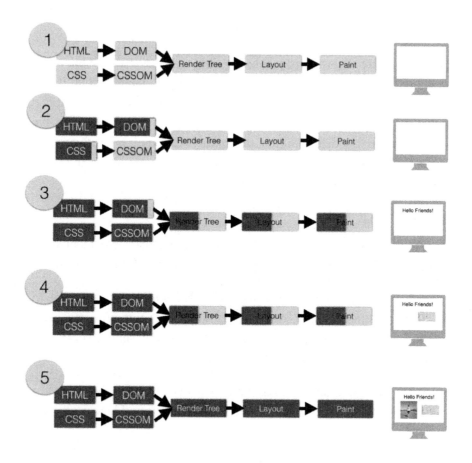

Figure 5.3. The critical rendering path

## Optimizing the Critical Rendering Path

We've just discussed how the browser works, what the CRP is, and what each step of the rendering process entails. Now let's apply this knowledge by identifying opportunities to optimize the CRP. Understanding how the browser constructs the CRP puts you at a huge advantage when planning how and what to load on your page. Anything that is not absolutely essential for serving the initial view of a page *should not* be on the CRP.

The goal is to improve the time to first render the page by prioritizing the visible content of the page. To optimize the CRP, first and foremost, you will need to minimize critical resources. In order to do that you will need to identify and remove render blocking assets as much as possible.

Latency is one of the biggest bottlenecks for serving fast websites. One way of helping to conquer this issue is to focus on visible (ATF) content first. If we can identify what is shown to the user above the fold in the browser, we can focus on that piece first when the page is loaded. Removing styles not needed for the ATF part of the page can drastically reduce the amount of time it takes to render the page. Since CSS is render blocking, anything that we can remove from the CSS will improve our render times.

## Follow the 14KB Rule

In the spirit of focusing on the visible content first, that also means focusing on the code that is at the top of an HTML page. Have you heard of the 14KB rule?

In Chapter 3, we discussed HTTP transactions. The first part of that is the initial connection. It's the time that the client and browser start to communicate, performing a "handshake". Each communication back and forth, before sending data, is defined as a **round trip**.

It is better to serve as much valuable content as you can within the first round trip. Having said that, only 14KB[2] of the HTML can be transferred before a new round trip.

We should therefore send the most critical data to render first—presumably the ATF content—within the first 14KB. This way we can avoid additional round trips in order to show the first bits and pieces of the page.

If you follow this 14KB rule, your Start Render time will be improved, as it will correlate with the first round trip time. Let's look at an example to check how the Start Render time plays out. I used the wrapper of my blog, and included several cute dog pictures. The page consists of a hero image (the wide image at the top), several dog images, and further down more styling, including the footer. The screenshot in Figure 5.4 displays the page with ATF content highlighted:

---

[2] http://storage.googleapis.com/io-2013/presentations/239-%20Instant%20Mobile%20Websites-%20Techniques%20and%20Best%20Practices.pdf

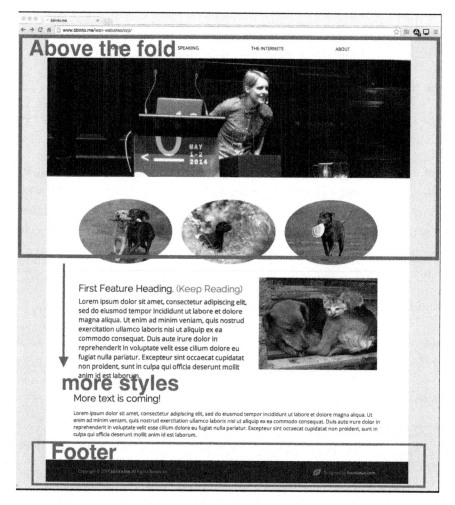

Figure 5.4. Our sample page, with the ATF area marked, as well as some additional styles outside the ATF

There are several tools available to help you extract styles for your ATF content from your style sheets, and instead embed (or "inline") them within the head of your HTML page. I used a bookmarklet[3] that was introduced by Paul Kinlan, a smart engineer at Google, to help me identify the critical ATF styles. You could also use the Critical Path CSS Generator[4] instead.

1. Load the page in a browser with the bookmarklet installed

---

[3] https://gist.github.com/terrencewood/8876579
[4] http://jonassebastianohlsson.com/criticalpathcssgenerator/

2. Click the bookmarklet, and voilà, the critical CSS appears in the console

4. Copy the output into the `head` of the page, wrapped in a `style` element

5. Move the rest of the CSS to the bottom of the page

Let's not stop here! Before I show you the result of the improvements thus far, I want to optimize the CRP even further by cleaning up the head.

You can do this by moving scripts to the bottom of the page and revisiting used style sheets. If you use different styles for different media (such as print vs. screen), make sure to use the `media` attribute to distinguish them. By specifying the `media` attribute for a print version of the page, you can be assured that the **print.css** style sheet won't be render blocking. However, note that the file will still be downloaded by the browser.

You *could* link to your print style sheet like this:

```
<link rel='stylesheet' href='http://www.bbinto.me/wp-includes/css/
➡print.css' type='text/css'/>
```

However, it's better to include the `media` attribute, as shown below:

```
<!-- print.css stylesheet is not render blocking -->
<link rel='stylesheet' href='http://www.bbinto.me/wp-includes/css/
➡print.css' type='text/css' media='print' />
```

Here was the head prior to cleanup. Quite messy, don't you think?

```
<head>
<meta charset="UTF-8" />
<meta http-equiv="X-UA-Compatible" content="IE=edge,chrome=1">
<meta name="viewport" content="width=device-width,
➡ initial-scale=1.0">
<link rel="shortcut icon" href="/favicon.ico" type="image/x-icon"/>
<title>bbinto.me</title>
<link rel='stylesheet' id='theme_stylesheet-css'  href='http://www.b
➡binto.me/wp-content/themes/matheson/style.css' type='text/css'
➡ media='all' />
<link rel='stylesheet' href='http://www.bbinto.me/wp-includes/css/
➡print.css' type='text/css' media='all' />
<link rel='stylesheet' id='google_fonts-css'  href='//fonts.googleap
```

```
➥is.com/css?family=Raleway|Open+Sans:400,400italic,700,700italic'
➥ type='text/css' media='all' />
<link rel='stylesheet' id='font_awesome-css'  href='http://www.bbint
➥o.me/wp-content/themes/matheson/library/css/font-awesome.css' type
➥='text/css' media='all' />
<style>
.boxed #page { max-width: 1172px; }
.container { max-width: 992px; }
</style>
<script type='text/javascript' src='https://ajax.googleapis.com/ajax
➥/libs/jquery/1.11.0/jquery.min.js'></script>
</head>
```

Moving unnecessary code out of the head to keep it as clean as possible will improve your loading time. Let's look at the cleaned-up head now:

```
<head>
<meta charset="UTF-8" />
<meta http-equiv="X-UA-Compatible" content="IE=edge,chrome=1">
<meta name="viewport" content="width=device-width, initial-scale=
➥1.0">
<link rel="shortcut icon" href="/favicon.ico" type="image/x-icon"/>
<title>bbinto.me</title>
<link rel="dns-prefetch" href="assets.dogtime.com" />
<link rel="dns-prefetch" href="fonts.googleapis.com" />
<link rel="dns-prefetch" href="google-analytics.com" />
<style> /* critical inline css */
*,::after,::before{box-sizing:border-box}*{word-wrap:break-word;outl
➥ine:0}html{font-family:sans-serif;font-size:62.5%;-webkit-tap-high
➥light-color:transparent}body{margin:0;font-family:'Helvetica Neue'
➥,Helvetica,Arial,sans-serif;font-size:14px;line-height:
...
</style>
</head>
```

Here is the footer:

```
<link rel='stylesheet' id='theme_stylesheet-css'  href='http://www.b
➥binto.me/wp-content/themes/matheson/style.css?ver=3.9.2' type='tex
➥t/css' media='all' />
<link rel='stylesheet' href='http://www.bbinto.me/wp-includes/css/
➥print.css' type='text/css' media='print' />
<link rel='stylesheet' id='google_fonts-css'  href='//fonts.googleap
```

```
➥is.com/css?family=Raleway|Open+Sans:400,400italic,700,700italic'
➥ type='text/css' media='all' />
<link rel='stylesheet' id='font_awesome-css'  href='http://www.bbint
➥o.me/wp-content/themes/matheson/library/css/font-awesome.css' type
➥='text/css' media='all' />
<script type='text/javascript' src='https://ajax.googleapis.com/ajax
➥/libs/jquery/1.11.0/jquery.min.js'></script>
```

It's show time. Let's check out the WPT video comparison to see the improvement:

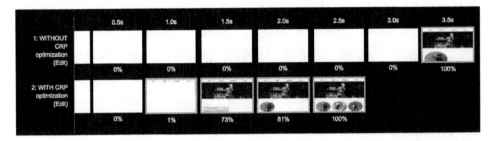

Figure 5.5. *WPT video comparison[5] of our sample page, showing before and after optimization*

| Test | Speed Index | Start Render | Visually Complete |
|------|-------------|--------------|-------------------|
| Without optimized CRP[6] | 3400 | 3.4s | 3.4s |
| With optimized CRP[7] | 1608 | 0.7s | 2.3s |

So to summarize what we've done for the page above:

- We focused on the order of rendering assets by loading critical assets as early as possible

- We kept scripts and styles in the head to a minimum, allowing only critical CSS in the head

- We kept the HTML as clean as possible

---

[5] http://www.webpagetest.org/video/compare.php?tests=141222_R6_JNC%2C141222_4C_KDV&thumb-Size=100&ival=500&end=visual#

[6] http://www.webpagetest.org/result/141222_R6_JNC/2/details/

[7] http://www.webpagetest.org/result/41222_4C_KDV/1/details/

- We moved non-critical scripts to the bottom of the page

# Reducing HTTP Requests

> The fastest HTTP request is the one not made. (Steve Souders, Chief
> Performance Officer at Fastly)

While you don't have a lot of influence over the user's network connection or the
server's processing time, you can optimize the things you do have control over—the
size and number of HTTP requests that are being sent.

The idea is simple: remove requests that you don't need to make, and think before
you include another HTTP request, especially if it's coming from a different domain
with an additional DNS lookup. For the requests you *do* need to make, you should
consider the following best practices.

## (Smart) Concatenation

A useful performance technique is to combine separate files into one, a process
called **concatenation**. With concatenation, you can reduce the number of HTTP requests and hence serve content faster.

Ideal candidates for concatenation are JavaScript and CSS files, as they make up
the bulk of the non-binary assets for a web page, besides the actual HTML itself.
Although concatenation can reduce the number of HTTP requests required, it doesn't
mean that concatenating absolutely everything into one big file is always the best
way to go. What you need is a smart concatenation strategy, as follows.

## CSS

First, create an inventory of all the CSS files used on your website. Go through them
and analyze which files would benefit from concatenation.

For example, assume you have a huge website with many style sheets covering the
styling of different pages. Concatenating numerous CSS files into one big consolidated CSS file might reduce the number of HTTP requests, but there are several edge
cases where this could actually result in overhead and redundancy:

- If one of these concatenated CSS files changes frequently, the browser would
  need to re-download the consolidated big CSS file every time it changes, which

is not optimal. One solution to this issue is to figure out which CSS files change infrequently versus the ones that changes frequently, and separate them accordingly.

- Figure out which styles are required on each page versus less frequently used styles. Every website should follow a style guide defining which colors and fonts to use on the site. For consistency, it makes sense to load these styles on each and every page of your website. However, there may also be styles that are not used on every single page. For example, it doesn't make sense to include the styling of a shopping cart page in the style sheet that is loaded on each page. The more selectors you put in your combined CSS file, the more complex and bigger it will be, which inevitably results in less performant code. Detach the uncommonly used styles from the commonly used styles. Before concatenating CSS files, ask yourself how often and under what circumstances those files are being used on the site.

## JavaScript

The same considerations about concatenation apply to multiple JavaScript files.

- Before merging one JavaScript file with another, think about the likelihood of the contents of both files changing. Are they changed equally as often? Evaluate if the content of these files should be fetched and cached separately by the browser, or combined into one single file.

- There might be functionality or widgets that are only used on certain pages of the site (for example, a photo gallery widget only showing up on one specific page of your website). There is no need to include them in the consolidated and concatenated master JavaScript file that is loaded on every page. The overhead of downloading unused JavaScript might be bigger than keeping files separated, especially if you know that not all visitors will need the gallery widget.

Make a conscious decision under what circumstances you should concatenate files. Ask yourself if the functionality executed in the JavaScript file is needed for all pages, or only for specific sections of the site.

Once you've figured out which files should be concatenated, you can then benefit from a performance gain. The following example illustrates the performance improvement that can be achieved when properly concatenating JavaScript files. The sample page relies on five separate JavaScript files—which should, therefore, be concatenated.

▨ **non-concat.html**: this file includes five JavaScript files:

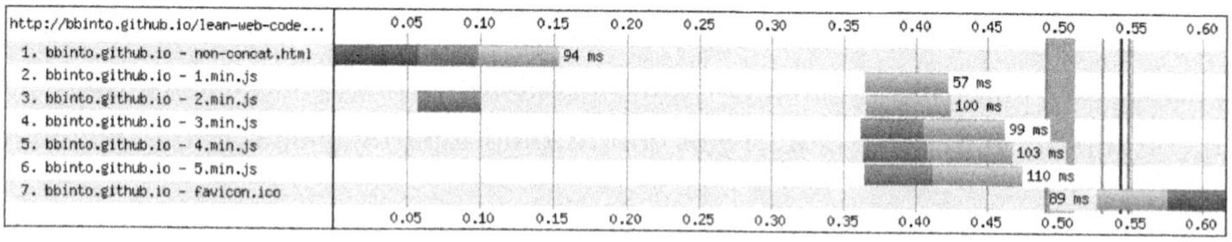

Figure 5.6. WPT Waterfall of non-concat.html[8]

▨ **concat.html**: this file includes the same JavaScript files concatenated into one JavaScript file, named **concat.js**:

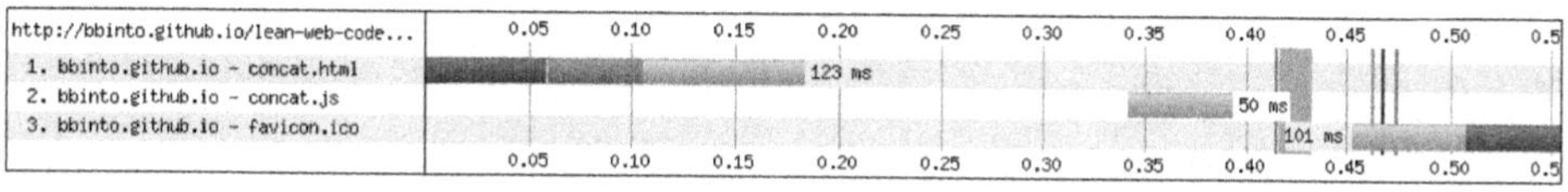

Figure 5.7. WPT waterfall of concat.html[9]

I ran both pages through WPT, focusing on Start Render and Fully Loaded values.

| URL | Start Render | Fully Loaded |
|---|---|---|
| non-concat.html[10] | 0.547s | 0.615s |
| concat.html[11] | 0.473s | 0.554s |

As you can see, there are some performance gains achieved by using concatenation.

## Conditional Loading

If you encounter styles and functionality that are not needed on every page, or for every browser, or even for every device, it's not recommended that their files be

---

[8] http://www.bbinto.me/lean-websites/chapter-5/minified/non-concat.html

[9] http://www.bbinto.me/lean-websites/chapter-5/minified/concat.html

[10] http://www.webpagetest.org/result/150117_KK_N3V/5/details/

[11] http://www.webpagetest.org/result/150117_NG_N3T/4/details/

concatenated. Rather, use conditional loading to load assets based on certain conditions and device features.

**Conditional resource loaders**, such as yepnope[12] and RequireJS[13], can help you load only the assets needed for your specific case. In addition, feature-detection libraries like Modernizr[14] can identify what capabilities and features the user's browser has, and therefore load or remove specific files. Detectizr[15], a library that sits on top of Modernizr, can trigger conditional loading based on the device.

## Tools

Though you can concatenate files by hand, it's preferable to use tools to automate this process. A quick solution is to use the **cat**[16] Unix command. For example, you can use the following command to concatenate all CSS files into **merge.css**, or all JavaScript files into **merge.js**:

```
$ cd css/
$ cat *.css > merge.css

// or JavaScript
$ cd javascript/
$ cat *.js > merge.js
```

There are also some more sophisticated command line tools available that combine concatenation and minification. Google's Closure Compiler[17] supports concatenation (only for JavaScript files), and task managers like Grunt[18] and Gulp[19] offer concatenation tasks and plugins as well. We will use Grunt and Gulp in Chapter 8 to show how to automate performance tasks.

---

[12] http://yepnopejs.com/

[13] http://www.requirejs.org/

[14] http://modernizr.com/

[15] https://github.com/barisaydinoglu/Detectizr

[16] http://en.wikipedia.org/wiki/Cat_%28Unix%29

[17] https://developers.google.com/closure/compiler/

[18] https://github.com/gruntjs/grunt-contrib-concat

[19] http://gulpjs.com/

Let's concatenate the files shown in the earlier example with Google's Closure Compiler[20]. Download the Java jar file[21] and execute one of the following commands:

```
java -jar compiler.jar --js_output_file=concat.js 1.js 2.js 3.js ...

# Recursively include all js files in subdirs
java -jar compiler.jar --js_output_file=concat.js 'src/**.js'
```

### No Java?

The local version of Closure Compiler requires the installation of Java and running it via the Java CLI runtime. If you don't want to use Java via a CLI, Closure Compiler is available online[22].

# Image Spriting

The main idea of **image spriting** is to reduce the HTTP requests that are needed to serve the images on the page. Spriting is done by combining each smaller individual image into one big image, and then displaying a small section of that image (a **sprite**) at defined X and Y coordinates. That way, instead of making multiple HTTP requests for each image, you'll only need one HTTP request.

Let's run through an example to show how it works. Say I have four flora images that I want to show on a page—a grass patch in a planter, a tree, a leaf, and a planted pot.

Instead of displaying each flora image by using separate image tags (and four HTTP requests) like this:

---

[20] http://closure-compiler.appspot.com/home
[21] https://code.google.com/p/closure-compiler/downloads/list
[22] http://refresh-sf.com/yui/

```
<img src="img/planter.png"/>
<img src="img/tree.png"/>
<img src="img/leaf.png"/>
<img src="img/pot.png"/>
```

we can create a sprite image using the CSS Sprites Generator[23], an online tool that allows you to upload each image individually, and which creates the required CSS as well as the sprite image (see below):

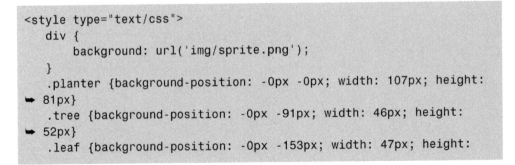

Figure 5.8. *Using the CSS Sprites Generator to create a sprite image and corresponding CSS*

We can now use the generated sprite image and the x/y coordinates to display each of the flora images in the page:

```
<style type="text/css">
    div {
        background: url('img/sprite.png');
    }
    .planter {background-position: -0px -0px; width: 107px; height:
➥ 81px}
    .tree {background-position: -0px -91px; width: 46px; height:
➥ 52px}
    .leaf {background-position: -0px -153px; width: 47px; height:
```

23 http://csssprites.com/

```
➡ 55px}
  .pot {background-position: -0px -218px; width: 42px; height:
➡ 79px}
 </style>
<!-- planter -->
<div class="planter"></div>
<!-- tree -->
<div class="tree"></div>
<!-- leaf -->
<div class="leaf"></div>
<!-- planted pot -->
<div class="pot"></div>
```

Let's check out these sample pages in WPT, first without using sprites (Figure 5.9) and then with sprites (Figure 5.10):

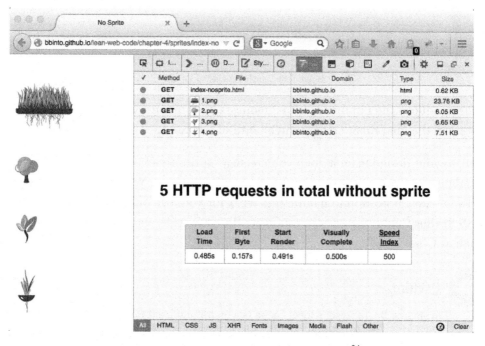

Figure 5.9. Sample page without sprites, using `img` tags[24]

---

[24] http://www.webpagetest.org/result/141108_DJ_K4M/

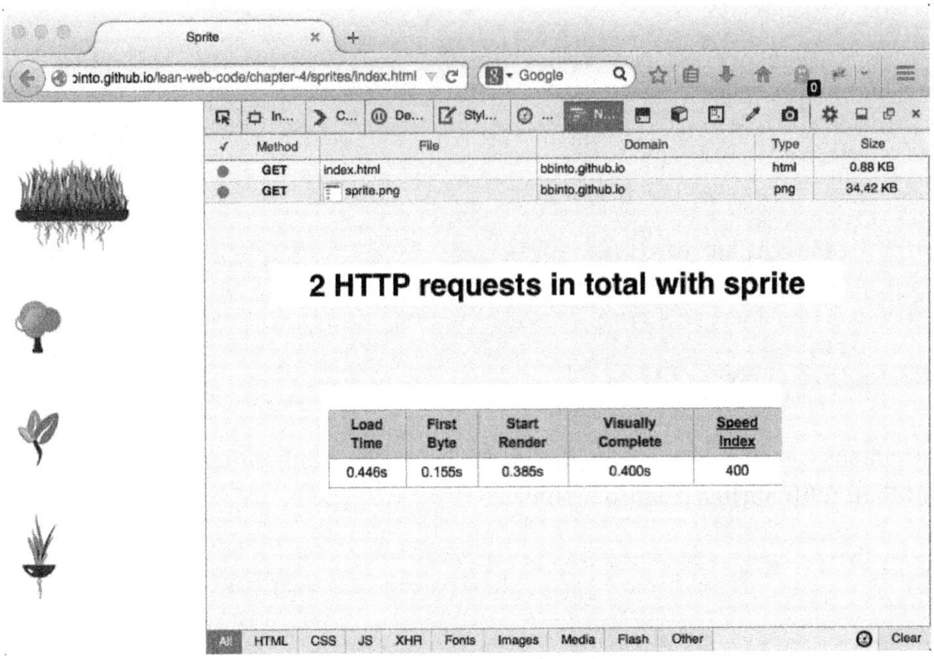

Figure 5.10. Sample page using sprites[25]

We've reduced the number of HTTP requests by three individual requests, and dropped the load time[26] by around a tenth of a second.

Talk to your design team to help you create a "sprite sheet". There are many[27] tools available that you or your designers can use for spriting. You can either write scripts[28] for Photoshop to handle this work for you, use online tools such as the CSS Sprites Generator, or even automate the process by using command line tools such as Glue[29].

## Caching

Leveraging the browser's local cache is a technique used for performance optimization. Every browser includes a cache, but needs to get instructions on how and when to use it. You can set the logic—such as when to request a newer or fresher

---

[25] http://www.webpagetest.org/result/141108_9F_K4F/

[26] http://www.webpagetest.org/video/compare.php?tests=141108_9F_K4F,141108_DJ_K4M

[27] http://blog.booking.com/automating-css-sprites-for-large-organisations.html

[28] http://www.johnwordsworth.com/projects/photoshop-sprite-sheet-generator-script/

[29] http://gluecss.com/

version of an asset, or when not to use the one in the cache at all—by using the `Cache-Control` headers.

We will learn more about caching and how to set `Cache-Control` headers to reduce HTTP requests in Chapter 9.

# Optimizing HTTP Requests

You can't remove all HTTP requests, as there are requests and assets that are crucial and required for the rendering your website. Therefore, after looking into how to avoid unnecessary HTTP requests, let's focus now on optimizing the requests that are absolutely necessary.

## Minifying

**Minifying** is the process of using a tool to eliminate unnecessary characters from your code to optimize it, without changing its functionality.

During the process of minifying, the following things are stripped out of your file:

- White space characters

- New line characters

- Comments

- Block delimiters

In addition to stripping out unnecessary characters, minifiers also typically rewrite sections of code (such as variable names or identifiers) to optimize it further. By minifying assets such as CSS, JavaScript or HTML files, you can significantly reduce the size of data that has to be sent over the wire, and hence improve load time and performance.

Closure Compiler, a tool we discussed earlier, not only provides concatenation capabilities, but also parses JavaScript, analyzes it, removes dead code and rewrites and minifies what's left.

> **Minify as a Final Step**
>
> Minification obfuscates the code, which thus makes it hard for humans to read. If your code is not yet production-ready and still needs some debugging, you might want to minify your code only during the last step of your deployment. Task runners, which I will introduce in Chapter 8, can add this kind of optimization as the last step of a build process.

## Tools

There are many online, browser-based tools available that help you minify your assets, such as JSCompress for JavaScript[30], CSS Minifier for CSS[31], and HTML Minifier for HTML[32]. The PageSpeed Insights plugin[33] for Chrome offers links to minified versions of your content, as shown in Figure 5.11:

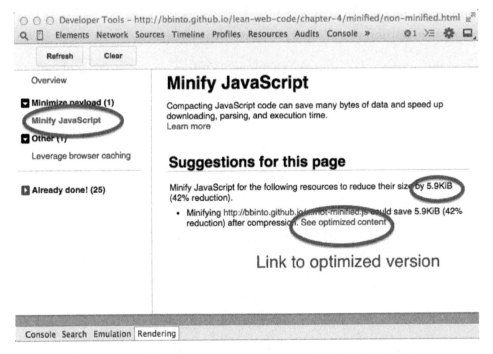

Figure 5.11. PageSpeed Insights Chrome plugin, offering minified versions of your assets

---

[30] http://jscompress.com/
[31] http://cssminifier.com/
[32] http://www.willpeavy.com/minifier/
[33] https://developers.google.com/speed/docs/insights/MinifyResources

In addition to the online tools and plugins, there are various command line tools that can be integrated into your deployment process—such as YUI Compressor[34], Closure Compiler, or JSMin[35]—to achieve the same outcome. We'll discuss the automation of these tools in more detail in Chapter 8.

Let's just take a quick look at YUI Compressor for now. After downloading the Java jar file[36], you can run the following command on CSS or JavaScript files to minify them. Please note that using this locally requires the installation of Java and running it via the CLI.

```
// minify all .css files in current folder, and save as -min.css
java -jar yuicompressor.jar -o '.css$:-min.css' *.css

// or simply
java -jar yuicompressor-1.0.jar -o 1.min.s 1.js
```

### No Java?

If you don't want to use Java via CLI, the YUI Compressor is available online[37].

# Pre-browsing

**Pre-browsing** is a performance optimization technique, and refers to an attempt to anticipate the user's interactions with your page—such as loading assets prior to the user requesting them. **Resource hints**[38]—which are pre-browsing attributes[39] added to the link tag—aim to help the browser predict your user's next steps by proactively telling the browser what to prefetch.

For example, you probably know where your users are headed most often on your site. You may be able to use some of the following options to preload certain resources that you know the browser will need to fetch for the next visited page.

---

[34] http://developer.yahoo.com/yui/compressor/

[35] http://www.crockford.com/javascript/jsmin.html

[36] https://github.com/yui/yuicompressor/releases

[37] http://refresh-sf.com/yui/

[38] http://w3c.github.io/resource-hints/

[39] https://docs.google.com/presentation/d/18zlAdKAxnc51y_kj-6sWLmnjl6TLnaru_WH0LJTjP-o/edit#slide=id.p19

Let's check out the resource hint attributes.

## rel="dns-prefetch"

As we saw earlier, DNS lookups can take up additional time to load assets. DNS prefetching reduces the time it takes to look up the domain by resolving it in advance.

DNS prefetching is useful when you have several links on your page referring to external websites (that is, pointing to different domains). It reduces latency when the user actually clicks on one of the external links. It's effectively telling the browser in advance, "Hey buddy, I'm planning to use this domain."

This tag should be placed in the head of your page, and only be used for critical resources with different domains. Don't include all the domains of your external links in the head, as this might only increase the page load time.

The example below adds DNS prefetching for the Flickr domain, as this domain is being used for images in a photo gallery, later on in the page:

```
<!DOCTYPE html>
<html lang="en">
<head>
    <link rel="shortcut icon" href="../../favicon.ico"
➡ type="image/x-icon"/>
    <!-- ... -->
    <link rel="dns-prefetch" href="https://farm3.staticflickr.com" />
    <title>My website</title>
</head>
<body>
    <!-- ... -->
    <img src="https://farm3.staticflickr.com/2076/2378396331_f550196
➡025.jpg">
</body>
</html>
```

## rel="subresource"

This resource hint allows pointing of the browser to another resource that you want to use later on in the current page, and which therefore should be downloaded as a high priority. Subresource resources are fetched with high priority as soon as they are encountered by the loader.

By using this resource hint, you can optimize the user experience on your site, as any resource marked as `subresource` is loaded faster. For example, this technique is very useful if you want to load resources such as important JSON files, or a logo, in advance.

Place this tag in the head of your HTML as early as possible. The resources fetched should just be critical resources for the **current** page. In the example below, it's a JSON file and a logo:

```html
<!DOCTYPE html>
<html lang="en">
<head>
    <!-- ... -->
    <link rel="subresource"  href="data.json" />
    <link rel="subresource"  href="logo.jpg" />
    <title>My website</title>
</head>
<body>

    <img src="logo.jpg"/>
    <!-- ... -->

    <script>
        $.getJSON( "data.json", function( data ) {
            //
        });
    </script>
</body>
</html>
```

## rel="prefetch"

You can hint to the browser that an individual resource—or an entire site—should be prefetched, by including the `prefetch` pre-browsing attribute in the head of your page. For example, you could use the prefetch hint to load images that are used throughout your site, and not just on your current page.

```html
<!DOCTYPE html>
<html lang="en">
<head>
    <!-- ... -->
    <link rel="subresource" href="logo.jpg" />
```

```
    <link rel="prefetch" href="footer.jpg" />
    <title>My website</title>
</head>
<body>
    <!-- ... -->
    <img src="logo.jpg"/>
    <!-- ... -->

    <img src="footer.jpg"/>
</body>
</html>
```

After the browser has dealt with all critical subresources, it will start getting **footer.jpg.** Please note that the prefetch hint is considered to be the lowest possible priority[40] hint.

Therefore, `subresource` and `prefetch` differ in their priorities as well as their semantics: use `subresource` to load a resource with high priority within the current page, whereas the `prefetch` resource is loaded with lower priority but can refer to a resource used on a different page of your site.

## `rel="prerender"`

With a use case similar to that of `prefetch`, `prerender` kicks off by loading an entire page in the background (including all of its assets). As I'm sure you can imagine, this event is quite resource heavy, and should only be used if it's really needed! You could use this for a checkout process, for example, where you can predict the subsequent pages the user will hit.

```
<!DOCTYPE html>
<html lang="en">
<head>
    <!-- ... -->
    <link rel="prerender" href="step-2.html" />
    <title>Check-Out Step 1</title>
</head>
<body>
```

---

[40] https://medium.com/@luisvieira_gmr/html5-prefetch-1e54f6dda15d

```
    <!-- ... -->
</body>
</html>
```

## Browser Support

Since some of these resource hint attributes are fairly new (at the time of writing), browser makers are still in the process of implementing them. Here's a table of current support:

| Browser | dns-prefetch | subresource | prefetch | prerender |
|---------|--------------|-------------|----------|-----------|
| Firefox | 3.5+ | n/a | 3.5+ | n/a |
| Chrome | 1.0+ | 1.0+ | 1.0+ | 1.3+ |
| Safari | 5.01+ | n/a | n/a | n/a |
| IE | 9+ | n/a | 10+ | 11+ |

As you can tell from the table above, `dns-prefetch` seems to be supported by most browsers—and therefore, if used properly, should improve a site's performance. Some external scripts could potentially have a long DNS lookup, so we could use this attribute to improve the load time.

# Cool Down

▓ You've learned how the browser works, so you understand when and how assets are being rendered.

▓ The CRP defines the resources that are needed to render the initial view of the page (above the fold).

▓ You've learned about the 14KB rule, and how to prioritize the visible content of your page.

▓ You've been taken through an exercise on how to optimize the CRP.

▓ Reducing and optimizing HTTP requests is the key for efficient web performance.

▓ You've learned techniques to reduce and optimize HTTP requests by applying concatenation and minification.

- Don't just concatenate everything. Differentiate between context-based and frequency-based concatenation.

- You've learned how spriting works, and that it reduces HTTP requests when serving images.

- You got a glimpse of how predictive browsing works, and learned about new tags for preloading assets—`pre-fetch`, `dns-prefetch` etc.

Chapter

# Producing Lean Web Assets: Part 1

## Warm Up

While the previous chapter explored techniques for reducing and optimizing HTTP requests in general, this chapter will focus on optimizing individual web assets such as HTML, CSS, and JavaScript.

## Optimizing HTML

When writing HTML, make sure it is semantic, valid, and as lean as possible. The more errors your code contains, and the more nested elements you have, the more work you are requiring of the browser. (The browser will do its best to correct your errors as it constructs the DOM, but there's only so much it can do.)

Move any inline styles from HTML elements into your style sheets. For example, instead of writing <div style="color:red">, use div {color:red} in a separate style sheet.

## Keeping Things Tidy

There are several tools that can help you keep your HTML in good shape, such as HTML Tidy[1], a command line tool that you can download from GitHub[2] and install on your computer. (There is also an older command line version[3], which has a handy online[4] equivalent, though these are a little old now and don't include support for HTML5.)

HTML Tidy not only checks your HTML for errors, but also warns of potential problems, and even produces an amended version of your file for you.

Another popular, online tool for checking the quality of your HTML code is the W3C Markup Validation Service[5]. You can provide it with a link to your page, upload a file or just paste your code straight into the form provided. The validator will list warnings and errors for you to address, although it won't rewrite your code for you.

## Further Tips on Optimizing HTML Files

Once your HTML code is error free, there are further ways to optimize it, such as the following:

- Reduce the file size as much as possible. Minify the HTML by removing whitespace and comments wherever possible. Instead of doing this manually, use compressors such as HTML Compressor, which has both a command line[6] and an online[7] version.

- Remove unused elements. As they serve no purpose, don't let the browser waste precious time processing them.

- Don't forget closing tags for elements that require them. The rendering step could stumble on this and get confused, potentially causing a delay (and a broken layout).

---

[1] http://www.html-tidy.org/
[2] https://github.com/htacg/tidy-html5
[3] http://tidy.sourceforge.net/
[4] http://infohound.net/tidy/
[5] https://validator.w3.org/
[6] https://code.google.com/p/htmlcompressor/
[7] https://htmlcompressor.com/compressor/

- Practice smart content layout. Place the most important content higher in the source order, letting less important content (such as sidebars) load further down the tree.

- Keep the head as small and clean as possible to prioritize visible content. The more links, scripts and other code in the head, the longer it will be before the browser can download the actual page content.

# Optimizing CSS

As we've discussed already, externally linked CSS files are render blocking. Each additional linked style sheet further degrades page load performance. Your rule of thumb should always be to send the most important styles down the wire as soon as possible, and inline styles in the head of the page itself if they apply above the fold.

## Lean CSS

Regardless of whether you use external style sheets or inline styles, aim to keep your CSS as lean as possible. In particular, avoid unused selectors. They will only bloat your style sheets and harm the load time of your page.

One of the key things to note when optimizing CSS is that browsers read CSS selectors from *right to left*. The part furthest to the right is the *key selector*, and is most responsible for the performance of the overall selector.

The most efficient selector is the ID, followed by class, tag, universal, attribute and pseudo class selectors. The efficiency is reflected by the order of occurrence of each selector below.

```
#content          {…}   /* ID */
body #title       {…}   /* ID */
.content          {…}   /* class */
ol li a.current   {…}   /* class *
ol                {…}   /* tag */
*                 {…}   /* universal */
[title='main']    {…}   /* attribute */
a:hover           {…}   /* pseudo */
```

By following the rules below, you ensure performant CSS:

▨ **Choose a specific key selector**. For example, the following key selector is not very efficient:

```
#menu a {…}
```

Based on the right-to-left principle, the browser must first find all existing links on the page before applying the style to the links found in the #menu element.

```
<ul id="menu">
    <li><a href="#">Home</a></li>
    <li><a href="#">Contact</a></li>
    <!-- more -->
</ul>
```

By adding a class to each <li> element, we can make the key selector more efficient:

```
<ul id="menu">
    <li><a href="#" class="menu-item">Home</a></li>
    <li><a href="#" class="menu-item">Contact</a></li>
    <!-- more -->
</ul>
```

The selector can now be optimized:

```
#menu .menu-item {…}
```

This optimized key selector will now match far fewer elements. The browser is able to find the elements faster, and can focus on the next styles to be rendered.

▨ **Remove unused selectors**. The older a style sheet is, or the more developers there are working on it, the more likely the file is to become messy and bloated due to unused selectors. (This could also happen for a CSS framework like Bootstrap, or in a CSS reset.)

▨ **Examine why you chose a selector in the first place**. It might not always be needed. In the case below, the font-family declaration cascades down, and there might not be a need to apply this to the li a:

```
#top-nav li a {font-family: Arial;}
```

You could clean this up as follows:

```
#top-nav {font-family: Arial;}
```

- **Avoid inline CSS**. Styles applied directly to elements via the `style` attribute are inefficient. Such styles should be moved to a style sheet instead, where they can potentially be reused. For example, the `style` attribute in `<header style="margin:5px; color:red"/>`, should be removed, in favor of this:

```
/* style.css */
header {margin: 5px; color: red;}
```

- **Consolidate declarations where possible**. Instead of duplicating the declaration `color: red;` as follows:

```
h1 {color: red;}
h2 {color: red;}
```

You can put this into one single rule:

```
h1, h2 {color: red;}
```

- **Be sparing with CSS3 selectors**. Although selectors such as `:nth-child` can be incredibly helpful in defining styles on specific elements of the page, they are the slowest when it comes to rendering time in the browser.

- **Avoid `@import url("style.css")`**. By using `@import`, the browser parses the CSS file and downloads each import file sequentially. To increase performance, use the HTML element `<link rel='stylesheet' href='style.css'>` instead of `@import`.

## CSS Optimization Tools

There are several tools that help with optimizing CSS, by removing unnecessary selectors, pointing out bad practices, and minifying your code:

- CSS Shrink[8] has an online and CLI version, and is useful for removing unnecessary selectors.

- Unused CSS[9] is an online tool for removing unused CSS.

- UnCSS[10] is a CLI tool for removing unused CSS.

- CSSLint[11] is an online tool that will "hurt your CSS feelings". It's brutally honest in pointing out any shortcomings of your CSS.

- CSSO[12] is a CLI tool that can minify and also perform structural optimization of CSS files.

If you want to carry out a quick optimization of some CSS, your best bet is to use the online tools above, or one of several browser extensions that are also available. For batched operations and automation, the command line tools are more useful during deployment. I recommend you take the time to set up these CLIs within your deployment process so that they are part of your daily workflow. In Chapter 8, we'll discuss how to set these up.

Let's take a look at CSS Shrink, to illustrate how a CSS optimization tool can help improve the performance of a site. I pasted the styles from one of my site's CSS files into the online version of CSS Shrink. As a result, my CSS was shrunk by almost 19%, as shown in Figure 6.1:

---

[8] http://cssshrink.com/
[9] https://unused-css.com/
[10] https://github.com/giakki/uncss
[11] http://csslint.net/
[12] https://bem.info/tools/optimizers/csso/

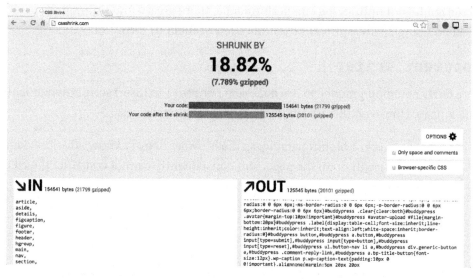

Figure 6.1. bbinto.me style sheet file size reduced by almost 19%, thanks to CSS Shrink

# Optimizing JavaScript

Inefficient JavaScript can have a big impact on a site's performance. JavaScript is render blocking if included synchronously, causing delays to page load if a script is inefficiently coded or simply too big. If the script appears in the `head` of the page, it will hold up the rendering of the critical page content. Therefore, put any scripts at the bottom of the page—just before the closing `</body>` tag—to avoid render blocking. Another option is to make the script non-blocking, by waiting until the `window.onload` event has fired before loading the rest of the JavaScript files, or by using the `async` and `defer` attributes. Both attributes prevent render blocking.

Another helpful approach is to use script loader libraries like RequireJS[13] to manage JavaScript dependencies.

## Lean DOM Operations

Any time you access the DOM with JavaScript, you will have to pay a performance price—especially when you actually modify the DOM via JavaScript. This is because the DOM sits outside the JavaScript virtual machine, meaning that changes to layout, compositing or painting are very expensive.

---

[13] http://requirejs.org/

In the context of optimizing site performance, there are several things to be careful of when using JavaScript. Let's examine each of them in turn.

## document.write()

It's a fairly common practice to use document.write() to insert scripts dynamically into a page. However, this creates several performance issues:

- document.write() blocks parsing, as the browser doesn't know what the document.write() will do to the page, and consequently cannot construct the DOM tree until it has run.

- Using document.write() messes with the browser's preload scanner[14], as it doesn't know about the code within document.write() yet.

- The document.write() code can only run during initial page parsing.

Where possible, use DOM manipulations instead of document.write().

## Loops

In the context of DOM manipulations, JavaScript loops can have a serious impact on page performance if not handled with care.

Loops run over and over again, so by improving how they run—and especially by improving anything in them that modifies the DOM—you can make big performance gains. See what kind of DOM operations are being executed in your loops, and investigate if you can move those DOM operations out of the loop. A good rule of thumb is to do as much work outside the loop as possible.

The following simple example illustrates how you can optimize a for loop and its content:

---

[14] http://andydavies.me/blog/2013/10/22/how-the-browser-pre-loader-makes-pages-load-faster/

```
var vals = [1,2,3,4,5,6,7,8,9,10];

for (var i=0; i < vals.length; i++){
    doStuff(vals[i]);
}
```

All items in the vals array are being passed into the doStuff() function. Can you see what's happening here? The length of the array is retrieved and recalculated on every execution of the loop to compare the iterator variable against the array length.

This is an inefficient and not performance-oriented practice, because the length of the vals array will not change during the loop's execution.

We can easily fix this by caching the length of the array in a local variable vals. Let's clean it up:

```
var vals = [1,2,3,4,5,6,7,8,9,10];

// Optimize by declaring a local variable for array length
var len = vals.length;

for (var i=0; i < len; i++){
    doStuff(vals[i]);
}
```

Now we have declared len as a variable, cached the length of the array, and thus don't have to recalculate the array length on every loop iteration. The local variable is now used for comparison, instead of using an expensive property lookup each time through the loop.

Declare local variables to store DOM references that you'll access repeatedly, especially when dealing with HTMLCollection objects, such as document.images. It's better not to hide all images in the DOM as follows:

```
for (var i=0; i < document.images.length; i++){
    document.images[i].style.display = 'none';
}
```

Every time the loop is executed and the code tries to access the document.images object, it's actually querying against the DOM for all nodes matching that type, resulting in an expensive property lookup. By keeping `document.images` in the condition of the loop, we add significant execution time to the loop.

A much better option is to cache the length in a local variable:

```
// Optimize by declaring a local variable for array length
var lenImgs = document.images.length;

for (var i=0; i < lenImgs; i++){
    document.images[i].style.display = 'none';

}
```

A simple change like this significantly reduces the efficiency and execution time of the loop.

## Repaints and Reflows

The render tree takes care of painting pixels onto the page. By repainting anything on the page, or triggering a reflow, you negatively impact the performance of your site.

### Repaint and Reflow Defined

Before we look at optimizing repaint and reflow, let's clarify what they are.

**Repaint**    Any time you change the style of an element in the DOM, the browser needs to **repaint** the page. This can happen, for example, if you change the background color of the page, or change the visibility of an element on the page. The browser engine needs to search through all the elements of the page to figure out what is visible and should be displayed. While this is expensive, it's not as expensive for performance as the next event: reflow.

**Reflow**    **Reflow** happens when the DOM tree is manipulated. This occurs every time layout and geometry change. For example, if you change the display, width, or height of an element—such as elements changing positions or sizes—visible DOM elements are added or removed, and font size or content changes occur. It's important to understand that a reflow of an element causes a reflow of all child elements *and* any elements following it in the DOM. Depending on the number and positions of reflows, this can result in a complete re-rendering of the page.

### Know Your Reflows and Repaints!

Check out CSS Triggers[15] for details on what element changes trigger repaint and reflows.

## Combining Repaints and Reflows into Batches

Both repaint and reflow are expensive operations and should be reduced and optimized as much as possible. If you really need to execute changes that could cause a repaint or reflow, try to combine them into batches, in order to apply them at once.

Let's look at an example where I modify a `div`'s look and feel:

```
<body>
<style>
    #info {display:none}
</style>
<div id="info">
    <h4>My Reflow Test</h4>
    <p><strong>Note:</strong> This is just an example</p>
    <h5>Unordered List follows:</h5>
    <ul>
        <li>List 1</li>
        <li>List 2</li>
    </ul>
</div>
</body>

<script>
function triggerReflow() {
    var findMe = document.getElementById('info');
    findMe.style.display = 'block'; // 1st. reflow
    findMe.style.background = 'yellow'; // repaint
    findMe.style.border = '1px solid black'; // repaint
```

---

[15] http://csstriggers.com

```
      findMe.style.fontSize = '10px'; // reflow
}
</script>
```

All `findMe.style` definitions trigger reflows on the `div` element, but also on all child elements.

Instead of executing reflows one by one, we should rather combine the styles and assign a class to the `div` as follows:

```
/* css */
.showme {
    display:block;
    background-color: yellow;
    border: 1px solid black;
}

// JavaScript
<script>
    function triggerReflow() {
        var findMe = document.getElementById('info');
        findMe.className = 'showme';
    }
</script>
```

## Improving Animations

Movement on the screen necessitates reflows and repaints. Animations in particular require the browser to do a lot of work, so it's important to make sure they are as efficient as possible.

**Animations and Frames per Second**

Animations are based on reflows, and the faster you execute the animations, the faster you will trigger them, and therefore, the faster they are finished. To create animations in JavaScript, you normally use the `setTimeout` or `setInterval` functions.

**Frame rate** is the rate at which a device produces consecutive images on the screen. The lower the frame rate, the more likely a user will see a "janky" experience, and conversely, the higher the rate, the smoother the experience of animation or scrolling. 60 frames per second (fps) is used as the standard value for most screens, as it matches their refresh rate (60Hz).

The smoothness of your animation depends on its frame rate. In order to accomplish a smooth experience for your users, make sure to keep the frame rate at 60fps. Otherwise, your users might experience your animations as clunky, especially when quickly scrolling up or down. The higher the frame rate, the more responsive the website feels to the user.

**requestAnimationFrame()**

requestAnimationFrame() is a native API that can execute any kind of animation in the browser—involving DOM elements, CSS, canvas, WebGL or anything else. It should be preferred over using setInterval() or setTimeout().

The difference between requestAnimation-Frame() and setInterval() or setTimeout() is that you tell the browser to draw the animation at the next available opportunity, and not based on a predefined interval that could take up more processing time and power. For example, set-Timeout() only refreshes the screen when it wants to, not when the computer is able to, and it doesn't care what else is happening in the browser—such as another browser tab being active instead.

requestAnimationFrame() groups all of the animations into one single browser repaint, resulting in fewer CPU cycles. Also, if you switch to a new tab, the browser will throttle the animation so you

> can visit other pages without the animation slowing down your browser.

So how do you optimize your page to avoid repaints and reflows, and make animations not feel "clunky" or "janky"?

You can't really remove all repaints and reflows, but you can try to minimize their occurrence. Here are some tips on how to optimize[16] them:

- Instead of using `setInterval()` or `setTimeout()` for animations, use `requestAnimationFrame()`.

- Avoid inconsistent frame rates, as this correlates with bad user experience. Either use 60fps or, if that's not possible, use 30fps consistently. `requestAnimationFrame()` can throttle animations, especially when the system can't handle rendering at the screen's refresh rate. A consistent 30Hz feels better to our eyes than 60Hz with some missing frames per second.

- Check your `onScroll()` handlers. This event handler can cause serious issues when scrolling. In general, adding too much stuff into JavaScript event handlers imposes challenges on the animation, especially when scrolling.

- Heavy CSS animations or drop shadows, blurs, linear gradients, also big fixed background images, can slow down rendering.

- Use animations on elements with position fixed or absolute. They won't affect other elements' layout, thus reducing the cascading effect that a reflow might otherwise trigger.

If you want to dig deeper how to optimize JavaScript, I highly recommend *High Performance JavaScript*[17], a book by Nicholas C. Zakas.

# Third-party Scripts

Recent investigation[18] has shown that the distribution of **third-party content** is growing. Ever more sites are using code and assets not hosted on their own domain.

---

[16] https://dev.opera.com/articles/efficient-javascript/?page=3#reflow
[17] http://shop.oreilly.com/product/9780596802806.do
[18] http://bigqueri.es/t/what-is-the-distribution-of-1st-party-vs-3rd-party-resources/100/3

In 2011, 32% of a site's content was coming from third-party content; by 2013, this had risen to 38%. While third-party scripts can be useful, when poorly implemented, their inclusion can have a significant performance impact.

> "In the strictest sense, anything served to the client that's provided by an organization that's not the website provider is considered to be third-party." — Ben Vinegar, author of *Third-Party Script*[19].

# Types of Third-party Scripts

There are several different categories of third-party content:

- **Advertising**: any advertising network or service offering JavaScript to be included in your page.

- **Tracking and analytics**: this includes tracking products such Google Analytics and Chartbeat.

- **Social media**: any social media scripts, such as those offered by Facebook, LinkedIn, Twitter and Google+.

- **Libraries and frameworks**: examples include jQuery, YUI, Twitter Bootstrap, or any helpers that are included on your page via their external hosts.

If you work for a company with a business intelligence, analytics or marketing department, the chances are high that you are being asked to include anything that could help measure the company's success. There is not one social media or tracking tool out there that marketing wouldn't like to try out. Social media, ads and tracking scripts are big temptations for marketers and companies wanting to better understand their customers or find other revenue streams. On the other hand, any foreign content you add on top of your own content—especially if it's JavaScript—will add weight and load time to your page.

However, your rule of thumb should be that the value you get from using a third-party script has to be greater than its performance hit.

---

[19] http://www.manning.com/vinegar/

# Content Overload

Check out the pie chart below, analyzing Wired.com[20]. It's not difficult to see that a significant amount of the content being provided is not coming from Wired.com:

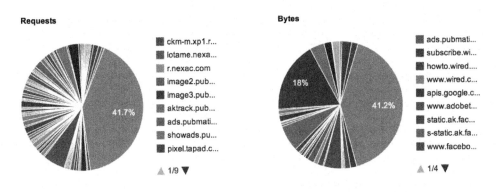

Figure 6.2. Wired.com content breakdown by domain

Considering that each additional external HTTP request costs another DNS lookup, this can result in significant latency issues.

### Ghostery

Ghostery[21] is a browser extension that lists all third-party scripts being used on a page. It can easily give you a quick idea of how much third-party content is adding to the page load time.

# Preparing for the Worst: SPOF

One of the most damaging things that can happen to your website is if a third-party provider goes down, and the script from that provider is included in such a way that it affects the critical rendering path. This worst case has a name: a **Single Point of Failure** (SPOF). SPOF describes an event where the entire system fails to execute. To quote Wikipedia[22]:

> A single point of failure (SPOF) is a part of a system that, if it fails, will stop the entire system from working. SPOFs are undesirable in

---

[20] http://wired.com
[21] https://www.ghostery.com/en/
[22] http://en.wikipedia.org/wiki/Single_point_of_failure

any system with a goal of high availability or reliability, be it a business practice, software application, or other industrial system.

## The Offending Tag

We've discussed the critical rendering path and how JavaScript blocks rendering.

```
<script src="http://example.com/3rdparty-script.js"></script>
```

If example.com were to go down, the entire content after this tag would be blocked from rendering. Imagine this tag sitting in the head of your page, blocking the entire content of the page below it. That's pretty bad. So what can we do to fix this?

## Avoiding SPOF

In this section, I'll describe a few ways to include scripts on a page and avoid the risk of SPOF events.

### The Dynamic Way

Have you heard of the dynamic script tag? It's been heavily promoted by Stoyan Stefanov—the man behind the performant Facebook Like button—and Philip Tellis, the creator of boomerang.js.

The idea is to asynchronously include a script, removing it from the critical rendering path and thus preventing it from blocking the rendering—when, for example, the host is slow to respond, or even down altogether. The browser downloads the script in the background, and once downloaded, executes it using the regular JavaScript thread:

```
1. <script>
2. (function(d,s,id){
3.     var js, 3js = d.getElementsByTagName(s)[0];
4.     if (d.getElementById(id)) {return;}
5.     js = d.createElement(s); js.id = id;
6.     js.src = "http://example.com.com/3rdparty-script.js";
7.     3js.parentNode.insertBefore(js, 3js);
8. }(document, 'script', '3rd-js'));
</script>
```

Let's look at this script line by line and see how it works:

■ **Lines 2 and 8**: this is an immediate, self-invoking function. We want to ensure that any temporary variable remains in the local scope and doesn't bleed into the global namespace of the host's page. We pass d, s, and id as arguments, since this is shorter than defining them in the body of the function.

■ **Line 3**: this line declares a variable and finds the first available <script> element on the page. That's the easiest hook for including the script on the page, as opposed to randomly appending it.

■ **Line 4**: this line checks if the script is already on the page, and if so, exits straight away, as there's nothing more to do, because we only need the file once. It prevents the script file from being included several times.

■ **Line 5**: this line creates a script element and assigns an id to it, so we can check for it later, and also to make sure it's not appended twice by mistake.

■ **Line 6**: here you point the src attribute of the script element to your third-party script.

■ **Line 7**: finally, we append the newly created script element to the DOM of the host page and we're done.

There are some drawbacks with this approach, though:

■ The script will still block on window.onload.

■ It also blocks the CSSOM (CSS object model), unless we place it before the CSS is loaded.

So is there anything better out there that we could use? Yes, there is!

### The Newer, Improved Way

Thankfully, more and more browser vendors have acknowledged the issue of loading scripts synchronously and blocking the rendering, so the W3C[23] has recommended two new attributes for the <script> tag. Without them, the browser runs the script immediately.

---

[23] http://www.w3.org/TR/html5/scripting-1.html

- `async`: when using this attribute, the browser loads the script when it's available, and won't block the DOM or CSSOM. It has an **unordered execution**, which means it can be placed anywhere on the page. This can be used for scripts that tolerate an out-of-order execution.

- `defer`: when using this attribute, the browser will run the script when the page has finished parsing.

With these new attributes, we can solve the following issues that the dynamic tag can't solve:

- The `async` attribute does not block the CSSOM.

- The preload scanner can only run on `src` and `href`, and hence can't preload anything that is defined as an inline script. Since the dynamic script tag is presented as an inline script, the scanner can't preload this piece.

Since these attributes are fairly new, only newer browsers support them, while older browsers won't know what they mean and will just ignore them. If your target audience uses IE8 and 9, or Android 2.2 or 2.3 devices, you might want to add `defer` to the tag, just in case, as `defer` was introduced prior to `async`. Use the combination of both attributes to cover a wider range of browsers[24], as suggested by the W3C.

## Tools for Fighting SPOF

Let's discuss a few tools and techniques for identifying potential SPOFs by collecting information about the third-party scripts on the page and how they've been included.

- **The SPOF-O-Matic**[25] **browser extension**: Pat Meenan, the creator of WPT, released SPOF-O-Matic, a useful Chrome extension. It detects potential SPOFs for a given page, and can simulate them as well. Using this tool to simulate SPOF will reveal how a website would render in case of a SPOF. It will help you detect if you've placed the script in your critical rendering path, or if the rendering of your page is unaffected by the third-party provider's code.

  Install the Chrome extension, browse to a site you'd like to "SPOF-check", and click the **SPOF-O-Matic** button as shown below:

---

[24] https://www.igvita.com/2014/05/20/script-injected-async-scripts-considered-harmful/

[25] https://chrome.google.com/webstore/detail/spof-o-matic/plikhggfbplemddobondkeogomgoodeg

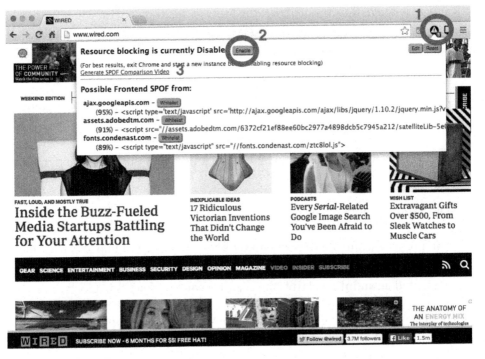

Figure 6.3. Screenshot of the SPOF-O-Matic extension in Chrome

As you can see in Figure 6.3, SPOF-O-Matic offers options to list all possible SPOF scripts (1), simulate SPOF via the browser (2), and to create a SPOF comparison video via WPT (3). I decided to "SPOF-check" wired.com because it relies on ads. As soon as the page is loaded, the extension indicates that there might be three scripts that could cause SPOF. Clicking on the badge opens up an additional window. It lists all scripts in detail. You can either choose to **Enable** SPOF via the browser and see the impact by reloading the page immediately, or by clicking the **Generate SPOF Comparison Video** link.

By clicking the link, you'll get redirected to WPT, where the scripts are already populated in a SPOF text box, located under **Advanced Settings**. When clicking **Start Test**, WPT will run the site with and without SPOF simulation, and will present you with a filmstrip, as shown in Figure 6.4:

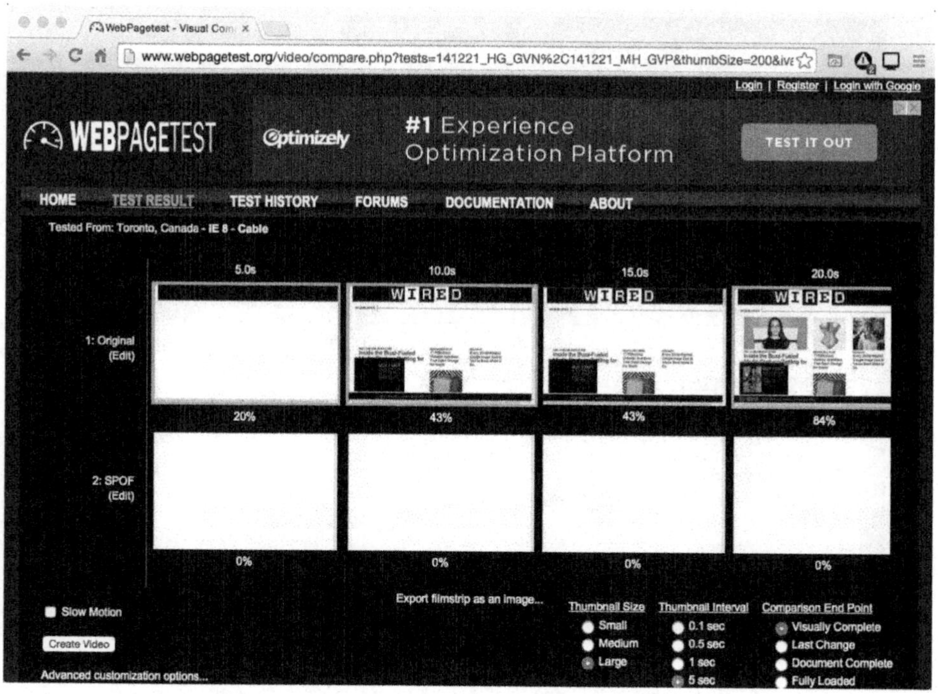

Figure 6.4. Filmstrip[26] of the SPOF simulation, including a link to the video comparison

If you want to record the filmstrip, click **Create Video** to report the test results as a handy video that can either be downloaded or embedded for future reference.

**SPOF simulator via WPT**: if you don't want to use the browser extension, you can use the SPOF functionality provided in WPT to simulate SPOF. WPT comes with a **SPOF** tab in its **Advanced Settings** that allows you to simulate SPOF for any given script. Just include the third-party script tags, and WPT will simulate what happens when this provider's site is down:

---

[26] http://www.webpagetest.org/video/compare.php?tests=141221_HG_GVN,141221_MH_GVP

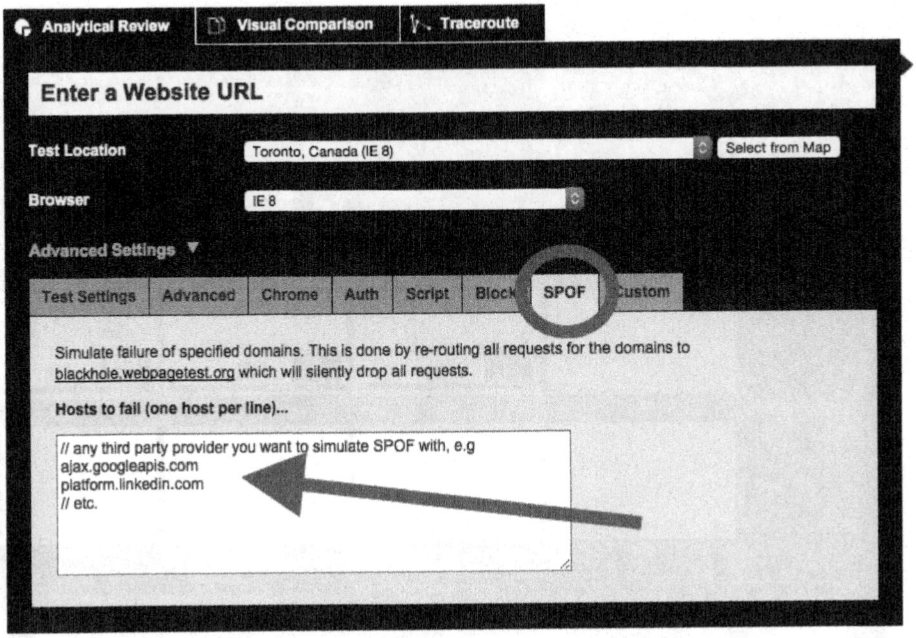

Figure 6.5. *Screenshot of WPT and the SPOF tab for including third-party scripts to test SPOF*

■ **Via blackhole in hosts file**: instead of using WPT, you can also simulate SPOF locally on your machine. Point the third-party domain to a blackhole[27]. The address for the blackhole is blackhole.webpagetest.org, with corresponding IP address `72.66.115.13`. It's a host with a firewall rule to drop all incoming packets, and hence simulates the host being down. Let's try it out:

   ■ Update the hosts file (please note you need to have administrator access to the machine to edit these files).

      ■ For Windows, the file is located under `C:\Windows\Sys-tem32\drivers\etc\hosts`.

      ■ On Mac, you can either use the Finder by clicking on Go -> Go to Folder in the Finder's menu, and pasting in `/private/etc/hosts`, or by typing in `vi /private/etc/hosts` in your preferred command line interface.

---

[27] http://blog.patrickmeenan.com/2011/10/testing-for-frontend-spof.html

First, use the blackhole IP address, followed by a space, and the third-party host address you want to simulate SPOF with.

```
72.66.115.13 www.google-analytics.com
72.66.115.13 connect.facebook.net
72.66.115.13 platform.twitter.com
```

■ On Mac, make sure to flush your DNS cache to apply the changes, typing `dscacheutil -flushcache` in the CLI. Restarting the browser will clear the browser's DNS cache as well.

■ Refresh the page in the browser and watch how the SPOF is being handled. Browse your site or others to see how they cope with any of these scripts being down.

# Tips for Working with Third-party Scripts

Let's summarize what we've discussed in this section. Next time you look into including any third-party scripts, consider the following tips:

■ In general, don't just copy and paste scripts. Make sure you know what they do, where to include them, and most importantly, why are they even being used.

■ Don't blindly use libraries and frameworks because they are convenient. Including little external helpers and libraries adds more HTTP requests to our page. Sometimes, we only need a fraction of what the library offers, and some specific functionality could easily be written by us—with fewer lines of code, and without an extra JavaScript include.

■ Make sure to allow yourself time to evaluate third-party scripts before including them. Verify if the provider cares about performance, or if they can even offer you help with including their scripts properly. Before choosing a provider, check if their code is concatenated and minified, and if they suggest asynchronous options for including the script. That should give you a good idea on where performance sits in their list of priorities. Google has released a list of third-party providers that offer asynchronous options. Review this list[28] to verify what providers play the proper performance game.

---

[28] https://developers.google.com/speed/docs/insights/UseAsync

- Put the risk and downtime of the third-party provider in the service level agreement (SLA). Make sure the agreement covers you for losses when the third-party provider goes down. This might encourage the provider to help you include the script in the most performant way.

### Choosing Third-party Providers

JS Manners[29] is a handy scoring system to help publishers choose the right third-party provider, based on specific performance characteristics.

# Cool Down

- You've received advice on optimizing HTML markup for performance, with tools such as HTML Tidy or HTML Compressor.

- You've been introduced to CSS best practices, and when and how to use different performance selectors. Remember, the most efficient CSS selector is the ID.

- Use tools such as CSS Shrink or CSSLint to help you identify non-performant CSS selectors.

- Performant JavaScript options have been presented to you. Avoid `document.write()` and expensive loops. Strive for lean DOM operations, and step back from repaints and reflows.

- You've learned how third-party content can be evil, and how, if it's not included properly, it could bring down your site. You've also been provided with options for including third-party scripts properly, such as circumventing the offending tag and using asynchronous loading options.

---

[29] http://jsmanners.com/

Chapter

# Producing Lean Web Assets: Part 2

## Warm Up

This chapter continues the theme of producing lean web assets, focusing on images, videos, audio, and web fonts. We'll cover several techniques for conquering common performance challenges with these assets, including when to use web fonts, and how to load them more efficiently.

> Webpages have to be designed with speed in mind. In fact, speed must be the overriding design criterion. To keep page sizes small, graphics should be kept to a minimum and multimedia effects should only be used when they truly add to the user's understanding of the information.

This comment comes from the Nielsen Norman Group[1] all the way back in 1997. But it's actually still a valid suggestion, even almost 20 years later: you should only include assets if they truly add value to your page.

---

[1] http://www.nngroup.com/articles/the-need-for-speed/

# Optimizing Images

Although images remain the main culprit for heavy and slow websites by having a proven high correlation to load times[2], they also offer some of the biggest opportunities for optimization.

First, let's have a look at the most common image formats, the average image sizes per page, and the median size of an image used on the top Alexa websites.

The most frequently used content type on the Internet is the image/* type. To further break it down, the most used image format is JPEG, followed by PNG and GIF, as shown in Figure 7.1:

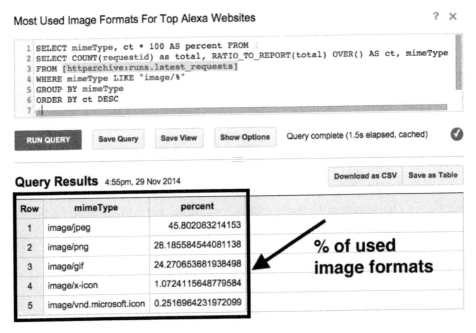

Figure 7.1. Big Query[3] result for most used image formats for top Alexa websites

The median image size used on the top Alexa websites was 30220 bytes, while the total image size per page averages at around 1206KB[4], as shown in the HTTP Archive pie in Figure 7.2:

---

[2] http://httparchive.org/interesting.php#onLoad

[3] http://bbinto.github.io/lean-web-code/chapter-7/queries/

[4] http://httparchive.org/trends.php

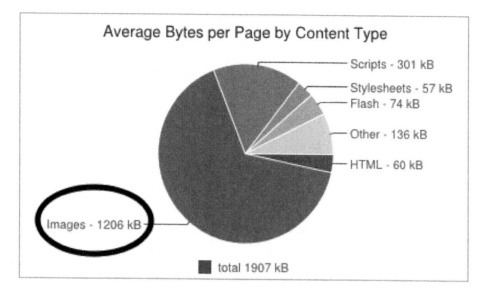

Figure 7.2. Average image size[5]

# Compression and Image Formats

The most efficient way to optimize images is to **compress** them. The idea behind image compression is to remove redundant image data. By doing so, the image size is dramatically reduced, and the asset can be served faster to the browser.

Image compression can either be lossy or lossless.

- **Lossy image compression**: the "lossy" filter *eliminates* some pixel data, mostly applied to photos.

- **Lossless image compression**: the "lossless" filter *compresses* pixel data—ideal for technical drawings, clip art, or comics.

Further, there are two approaches to encoding image data—raster and vector graphics, which are covered next.

---

[5] http://httparchive.org/trends.php

## Raster Graphics

**Raster** graphics represent an image by encoding the individual values of each pixel within a rectangular grid. The following image formats fall under the category of raster graphics:

| Format | Compression | Description |
|---|---|---|
| JPEG[6] | Lossy | Best choice for photos or screenshots, though not recommended for logos or line art. |
| JPEG2000[7] | Lossy and Lossless | Its biggest advantage over JPEG is that it offers lossy and lossless compression. Has the ability to deliver much smaller files but the same level of detail as JPEG. |
| Progressive JPEG[8] | Lossy | Loads in a series of scans, starting with a low-resolution version, with several versions in between until the full resolution has been achieved. |
| GIF[9] | Lossless | Only supports 256 colors. Use instead of JPEG if you only need a few distinct colors, or need to create text images. Allows transparency, but is mostly known nowadays |

[6] http://en.wikipedia.org/wiki/JPEG
[7] http://en.wikipedia.org/wiki/JPEG_2000
[8] http://en.wikipedia.org/wiki/JPEG
[9] http://en.wikipedia.org/wiki/Graphics_Interchange_Format

| Format | Compression | Description |
|--------|-------------|-------------|
|  |  | for its support for animations. |
| PNG[10] | Lossless | Can be 5%–25% more compressed than GIF. Also supports transparency. Use over GIF if you need to preserve a lot of colors. Can be much smaller than JPEG or GIFs, and hence is a preferred format to display text images or logos. PNG-8, similar to GIF, can support up to 256 colors, whereas PNG-24 is able to display millions of colors. |
| WebP[11] | Lossy and Lossless | Another web image format, developed by Google, promising 45% more compression than PNG. It's not supported by all browsers yet. We'll discuss this later. |

### Progressive Images

It might seem obvious that progressive image rendering would improve perceived load time[12], because users receive visual feedback faster than with a regular JPEG image. However, a study[13] by Radware suggests that progressive images actually harm perceived performance by increasing user frustration.

---

[10] http://en.wikipedia.org/wiki/Portable_Network_Graphics
[11] http://en.wikipedia.org/wiki/WebP
[12] http://calendar.perfplanet.com/2012/progressive-jpegs-a-new-best-practice/
[13] http://t.co/uDgtM2fFjv

## Vector Graphics

**Vector** graphics are created from lines, points, and polygons. Vector graphics don't lose quality when resized, whereas raster images become pixelated when you zoom in on them.

The standard vector format for the web is Scalable Vector Graphics (SVG). Behind the scenes, they are written in XML, and you could create them by hand. More commonly, though, programs such as Adobe Illustrator and Corel Draw are used to create and export them for the web.

You can even animate SVGs with JavaScript, but as always, consider how much real value this adds to your pages before weighing them down with extra code.

As with raster images, SVGs can be optimized for fast loading by minimizing the amount of data they contain. (For example, you may be able to remove lines and points without reducing the quality of the graphic.) Again, you can optimize an SVG manually, but it's more commonly done with various tools (some of which are listed below). For further information on the performance of SVG images, check out the 2014 Performance Calendar article[14] by Sara Soueidan.

## When to Use What?

In general, raster graphics should be used for complex scenes with detailed shapes or forms, such as photorealistic images. Vector graphics are suitable for images that consist of geometric shapes, such as logos. The advantage of vector graphics is that they can be zoomed to any size without reducing the quality.

From a performance perspective, it mostly comes down to the file size of each individual format. The file size for vector graphics is typically small, making them a perfect fit for both multi-device and high-resolution screens.

# Image Compression and Optimization Tools

Once you've decided on a format for your images, you can optimize them through compression. The following table lists some useful, open-source tools for this purpose. Most of them can run from the command line.

---

[14] http://calendar.perfplanet.com/2014/tips-for-optimising-svg-delivery-for-the-web/

| Tool | Compression | Supported Formats |
|---|---|---|
| Kraken.io[15] | Online service, with a limited, free online version, plus a paid Pro version with more features, including an API. | PNG, GIF, JPEG, SVG |
| Compressor.io[16] | Online service. | PNG, GIF, JPEG, SVG |
| jpegtan[17] | CLI for lossless optimization (including the removal of EXIF[18] meta data, such as camera information etc.). Removing EXIF data can reduce the file size of your image. | JPEG |
| optipng[19] | CLI for lossless compression of PNG, also for converting other formats to PNG. | PNG |
| pngquant[20] | CLI for lossy compression of PNG images. | PNG |
| gifsicle[21] | CLI for creating and optimizing (animated) GIFs. | GIF |
| Trimage[22] | CLI for lossless compression, and | PNG and JPEG |

[15] https://kraken.io/
[16] https://compressor.io/
[17] http://jpegclub.org/jpegtran/
[18] http://en.wikipedia.org/wiki/Exchangeable_image_file_format
[19] http://optipng.sourceforge.net/
[20] http://pngquant.org/
[21] http://www.lcdf.org/gifsicle/
[22] http://trimage.org/

| Tool | Compression | Supported Formats |
|------|-------------|-------------------|
|  | removing EXIF and other metadata. |  |
| ImageMagick[23] | CLI for lossless optimization. | Over 100[24] |
| ImageOptim[25] | Stand-alone app or CLI for lossless optimization and removing unnecessary color profiles and other metadata. | PNG, GIF, JPEG |
| Scour[26] | CLI for cleaning and optimizing SVGs. | SVG |

While online tools and browser extensions are useful for occasional optimization tasks, the command line tools can be used for batch processing and automation during deployment. (See Chapter 8 for more on automation).

# Data URIs

Data URIs provide another interesting option for including images on your page. What looks like an image to you just looks like a long string of letters and numbers to a computer. That long string is called a **data URI**.

A data URI is a Base64[27] string. (Base 64 is an encoding scheme that represents binary data in an ASCII string format.) Once you've converted your image to a data URI, you can insert that string straight into your HTML or CSS—thus saving your browser one HTTP request, which normally also means improving your site's performance.

---

[24] http://www.imagemagick.org/script/formats.php

[23] http://www.imagemagick.org

[25] https://imageoptim.com

[26] http://codedread.com/scour/

[27] http://en.wikipedia.org/wiki/Base64

Let's use a **leaf.png** example image to show how to convert it to a data URI. There are lots of tools for performing the conversion. I used DATAURL.NET[28], as shown in Figure 7.3:

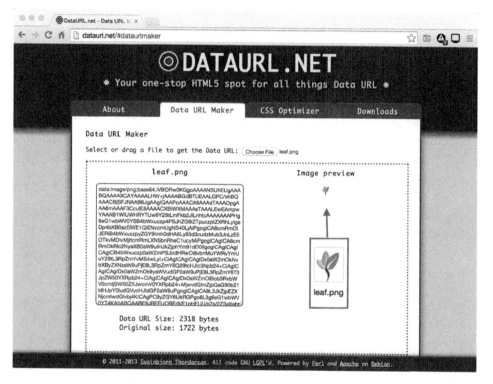

Figure 7.3. Converting a PNG image to a data URI

Here's a trimmed version of the output:

```
data:image/png;base64,iVBORw0KGgoAAAANSUhEUgAAABQAAAAXCAYAAAALHW+jAA
"AABGdBTUEAALGPC/
        xhBQAAACBjSFJNAAB6JgAAgIQAAPoAAACA6AAAdTAAAOpgAAA6mAAAF3Ccu
        ....
        +7Qwdz8SrsdYz2s7ee7rLc2M4qVcD23mRbJpOB3+fDnr17bT+bgBNTHS+y
"oNqFcVw2CzPTO/rQN+/erQOVRpu9bs3+BwJLmvcQyqFgAAAAAE1FTkSuQmCC
```

You can either put this code inside a style sheet or in an image tag in your HTML.

1. Data URI via the `<img>` tag:

---

[28] http://dataurl.net/#dataurlmaker

```
<img src="data URI output" />
```

2. Via external or inline CSS:

```
.mydatauri {
    background:url(data URI output)
}
```

You can either use online tools to create data URIs as shown above, or use CLI tools. For example, you could use CSSEmbed[29] via the Java CLI runtime. This tool looks through your CSS file and converts all images to base64 encoded strings within your CSS. For example, consider this CSS:

```
/* style.css */
background: url('leaf.png');
```

By running the jar file, **leaf.png** will be converted to a data URI image.

```
java -jar cssembed.jar -o style_optimized.css styles.css
```

The new styleheet is outputted as follows (trimmed):

```
/* style_optimized.css
background:url(data:image/png;base64,iVBORw0KGgoAAAANSUhEUgAAABQAAAA➡
XCAYAAAALH
+jAAAABGdBTUEAALGPCxhBQAAACBjSFJNAAB6JgAAgIQAAPoAAACA6AAAdTAAAOpgAAA
...)
```

It's worth noting that base64 encoding makes file sizes roughly 33% larger[30] than their original binary representations. Therefore, it's better to use the data URI format on smaller images rather than on larger ones, as it could worsen the performance of your page. And of course, optimize your image as much as possible *before* converting it to a data URI.

---

[29] https://github.com/nzakas/cssembed/downloads/

[30] http://davidbcalhoun.com/2011/when-to-base64-encode-images-and-when-not-to/

Also, watch out for caching limitations. Data URI images become part of a larger HTML or CSS file, so to cache images encoded as data URIs, we need to cache the pages that contain them. So, for example, if you put data URI images in your HTML, they can only be cached as defined by the HTTP cache control header (we'll discuss caching in more detail later). If the HTML is not cacheable, the entire content of the HTML markup—including the inline data URI—will need to be re-downloaded every single time a user visits the page. That can worsen performance if the image is large. Hence, one option is to put the encoded image in your style sheet, as you can then have a more aggressive cache for the CSS file, while the HTML page can have no-cache or a very limited cache, as HTML content is more likely to change. Large images make this more of a problem, so a useful rule of thumb is to not inline any asset that is bigger than 4KB.

# WebP

WebP is a relatively new image format that promises great file size savings over PNGs and JPEGs.

WebP[31] is an open-source image format, only currently supported in Chrome, Opera, and Android. Some notable websites such as Facebook have started to adopt this format[32] with great success. Most images sent to Facebook and Messenger for Android use the WebP format, which has resulted in data savings[33] of 25–35% compared to JPG, and 80% compared to PNG.

You can convert your images to WebP using a converter. I used ImageMagick[34] to convert `leaf.png` to WebP, by installing ImageMagick and running the following command:

```
convert leaf.png -quality 50 -define webp:lossless=true leaf.webp
```

You can tweak the settings by adding additional options[35].

[31] https://developers.google.com/speed/webp/?csw=1

[32] http://highscalability.com/blog/2014/9/22/how-facebook-makes-mobile-work-at-scale-for-all-phones-on-al.html

[33] https://code.facebook.com/posts/485459238254631/improving-facebook-on-android

[34] http://imagemagick.org/

[35] http://www.imagemagick.org/script/webp.php

One of the drawbacks of WebP is that not all browsers support this new format, notably Firefox, Internet Explorer and Safari. So you'll need to save two versions of the image, one in WebP and one in the legacy image format, which will take more storage space on your server.

While it's recommended to experiment with different quality settings, as well as compression options, to verify which image format is smaller and comes with less detail loss, WebP will outperform JPEG and PNG files for size most of the time. Even with comparable quality levels, WebP images are significantly smaller[36].

We've gone over several image formats and techniques now. Let's see how they all compare with each other.

## Comparison of Image Formats

I ran a performance test where I compared the following formats for the previously used leaf image[37].

I used a vector-based source file of 180x180px and saved it to PNG, SVG, WebP, and created a data URI from the PNG.

1. Inline Data URI[38]: base64 encoded image included inline as an image via <img>:

```
<img src="data:image/png;base64,iVBORw0KGgoAAAANSUhEUgAAALQ..."/>
```

2. WebP[39]: PNG converted into WebP with ImageMagick, and referenced as a background image via external CSS:

```
/* style.css*/
.leanleaf{
    background-image: url(../img/leaf.webp);
    /* ... */
}
```

---

[36] https://www.andrewmunsell.com/blog/jpg-vs-webp

[37] http://www.vectorvaco.com/grass-and-green-vector-13164/

[38] http://www.bbinto.me/lean-websites/chapter-4/data-uri/data-uri-inline/

[39] http://www.bbinto.me/lean-websites/chapter-4/data-uri/webp/

3. SVG[40]: exported vector-based source file to SVG, included as a background image via an external CSS file:

```
/* style.css*/
.leanleaf{
    background-image: url(../img/leaf.svg);
    /* ... */
}
```

4. Data URI[41]: base64 encoded and included as a background image in an external CSS file:

```
/* style.css*/
.leanleaf{
    width:156px;height:169px;background:url(data:image/png;base64,
➥iVBORwOKGgoAAAANSUhEUgAAALQAAAC0CAYAAAA9zQYyA...)
➥ no-repeat;margin:auto auto;}
```

5. PNG[42]: PNG image, referenced as a background image via external CSS:

```
/* style.css*/
.leanleaf{
    background-image: url(../img/leaf.png);
    /* ... */
}
```

After creating the sample pages, I tested the load times and file size of each page.

To get some representative performance data, I used phantomJS[43] to record the load time measurements for each example page (100 data points each).

---

[40] http://www.bbinto.me/lean-websites/chapter-4/data-uri/svg/

[41] http://www.bbinto.me/lean-websites/chapter-4/data-uri/data-uri-external

[42] http://www.bbinto.me/lean-websites/chapter-7/data-uri/png-css

[43] http://phantomjs.org/

| Result | Inline Data URI | WebP | SVG | External Data URI | PNG |
|---|---|---|---|---|---|
| Median (ms) | 142.5 | 179 | 216 | 258 | 282 |
| HTML size (bytes) | 9873 | 1769 | 2161 | 10085 | 1959 |

Inline data URI and WebP show the fastest median load times, whereas PNG as a CSS background image loads the slowest, followed by the data URI in CSS and the SVG served via CSS.

If you're not sure what format is going to give the best performance for your site, try collecting some load time data first, to see what format proves to be the most performant.

# Optimizing Video

Like images, video files tend to be bigger than CSS, JavaScript, or HTML files, so they come with a higher performance price, though they can also add value to your site.

Your videos should be encoded to play on as many devices as possible, but also should be no larger than necessary. Many of your users may have slow download speeds and expensive data plans. Several of the top Alexa websites use auto-playback for videos on their landing page, leaving a huge performance footprint for visitors—which results in many "F" marks in WPT[44].

Video file size is dependant on frame and bit rate, resolution, compression format, and delivery method. In this section you'll learn how to optimize these factors.

## Video Creation and Content

The more complex a video is, the harder it is to compress, which makes it more difficult to optimize. If you have control over how the video is shot, there are steps you can take to ensure that the video will be easier to compress:

- Aim for noise-free content.

---

[44] http://www.webpagetest.org/result/141028_30_CJV/

▨ Keep the number of zooms to a minimum.

▨ Keep the number of background details and movements to a minimum.

> ### 📝 Audio
>
> Studies[45] have shown that audio quality can affect *perceived* video quality. This means that if you have good-sounding audio, people will think your video *looks* better. That said, if your video uses mostly spoken words, and no music, you should be fine[46] using mono rather than stereo audio (which will save some bandwidth that can be allocated to the video instead).
>
> Audio bit rates should be defined[47] based on their content, and therefore only set as high as your content demands. Rates between 64 and 128kbit/s are sufficient for most cases. For recording human speech, a low bit rate of around 64kbit/s is acceptable. For music audio, a higher bit rate of 192kbit/s would be ideal.

# File Size: Frame Rate, Bit Rate, and Resolution

Video settings including frame rate, bit rate and resolution, each of which affects the file size of a video.

**Frame Rate**    The **frame rate** is defined as the number of frames that appear every second. It's measured in frames per second (fps). The higher the frame rate or resolution, the better the video experience for the user.

However, every tweak to increase the frame rate will increase the overall file size—so it's important to identify what the intention of your video is. For example, if you record a PowerPoint presentation with very little movement but you care about image quality, you might want to focus more on higher resolution and lessen the frame rate. For fast-moving recordings, such as sports events, you'll want to make sure to capture as many frames[48] per second as possible, while giving up a bit of your resolution in return.

---

[45] http://web.media.mit.edu/~vmb/papers/russ_sound.pdf

[46] https://ustream.zendesk.com/entries/22962268-Encoding-Specs-and-Stream-Settings#bandwidth

[47] http://support.video.limelight.com/support/docs/encoding_guide/

[48] https://ustream.zendesk.com/entries/22962268-Encoding-Specs-and-Stream-Settings#recommended

| | |
|---|---|
| **Resolution** | There are two common **resolution** formats—standard definition (SD) and high definition (HD). Most common resolutions for SD videos include 640x480px (4:3 aspect ratio) and 640x360px (16:9 aspect ratio). HD video is usually formatted at 720p (1280x720px) or 1080p (1920x1080px).<br><br>Obviously, the higher the resolution, the greater the file size of a video, and the longer it will take to deliver to your online consumers. |
| **Bit Rate** | The **bit rate** controls the visual quality of the video and the file size, measured in kilobits per second (kbit/s). Adobe[49] recommends lower bit rates for videos delivered over the web. Depending on the resolution, the following bit rates could serve as a guideline[50]: for SD, use 2,000–5,000kbit/s; for HD, use 5,000–10,000kbit/s for 720p, and 10,000–20,000kbit/s for 1080p. |

# Containers, Codecs and Compression

Once you've selected the frame rate, resolution and bit rate, you'll need to render the video to a specific video format. These formats are also called **video containers**. Video containers contain codecs, so the video player knows how to read and play the file.

## Containers

The most common video formats are shown below:

| Format | Description |
|---|---|
| .mp4[51] (H.264 encoded) | Used for YouTube and Vimeo videos. No default video player on Windows can play the file format. Tools such as VLC are required for playback. |

---

[49] http://help.adobe.com/en_US/mediaencoder/cs/using/WSb8e30982e628fbecc0e59e6131255b4dd2-8000.html#WSb8e30982e628fbecc0e59e6131255b4dd2-7ffd

[50] https://vimeo.com/help/compression

[51] http://en.wikipedia.org/wiki/MPEG-4_Part_14

| Format | Description |
|--------|-------------|
| .mov[52] (H.264 encoded) | No default video player on Windows can play the file format. Tools such as VLC are required for playback. |
| .wmv[53] | No default video player on Mac can play the file format. Tools such as VLC are required for playback. |
| .flv[54] | Flash player required, not supported by all devices (e.g. iOS). |
| .ogg[55] | Open-source, candidate for HTML5 video format. |

## Codecs and Compression

The **codec** determines how the video is **co**mpressed and **de**compressed (hence the name **codec**). Part of that process is determining the complex relationship between bit rate and resulting quality.

Have you ever tried to export a video you created with iMovie? There are many settings you can choose, because there are lots of video and audio codecs available. These are some common ones:

- H.264[56]: video encoding standard for Blu-ray discs, Vimeo, YouTube and the iTunes store. The intention of this codec is to provide good video quality with low bit rates. It's also the most used video codec today for mobile and web, providing small file sizes but higher quality video than other codecs (e.g. Sorensen Spark[57], Google's On2) while still having the same bit rate.

- MP3 (MPEG-1 Audio Layer 3[58]): MP3 is the most popular audio codec. For compatibility reasons, and due to its age, MP3 has been the most commonly

---

[52] http://en.wikipedia.org/wiki/QuickTime
[53] http://en.wikipedia.org/wiki/Windows_Media_Video
[54] http://en.wikipedia.org/wiki/Flash_Video
[55] http://en.wikipedia.org/wiki/Ogg
[56] http://en.wikipedia.org/wiki/H.264/MPEG-4_AVC
[57] http://en.wikipedia.org/wiki/Sorenson_Media#Encoding_Technologies
[58] http://en.wikipedia.org/wiki/MP3

supported audio codec. However, if you choose purely by quality and performance, you'd want to go with AAC+.

- AAC+ (Advanced Audio Coding[59]): AAC+ is an audio codec that offers the best audio quality at low bit rates. It's used by YouTube, iPhone, PlayStation, Android, Blackberry etc.

# Delivery Method

Common delivery methods for videos over the web include streaming, download, and progressive download. Based on the file size and bandwidth, you'll get different performance results for different user scenarios.

## Streaming

**Streaming** is achieved using a streaming protocol where the streamed video is watched from within the browser. Streaming can also be cacheless, allowing the streaming publisher to make it more secure and not easy to store locally. Two of the most well-known examples for streaming video services are YouTube and Vimeo.

There are two main protocols for streaming web video content. Both of them focus on bandwidth optimization, and are delivered by dedicated streaming servers.

- RTMP (Real Time Messaging Protocol[60]) is older and runs on port 1335, meaning that it potentially won't be viewable by visitors who only have port 80 open (HTTP). It was developed by Macromedia (now Adobe) to stream audio, video and data over the Internet for Flash players.

- A more common streaming solution offers HLS (HTTP Live Streaming[61])/HDS (HTTP Dynamic Streaming[62]). The video stream is split up into timed chunks (usually 10 seconds). The browser makes a regular HTTP request for each chunk of data. This means that the same optimization rules apply here as for other assets such as CSS and HTML. For example, caches can take advantage of the chunked discrete data and cache video streams for multiple users—something you can't do with RTMP.

---

[59] http://en.wikipedia.org/wiki/Advanced_Audio_Coding
[60] https://www.adobe.com/devnet/rtmp.html
[61] http://en.wikipedia.org/wiki/HTTP_Live_Streaming
[62] http://www.adobe.com/ca/products/hds-dynamic-streaming.html

## Download

**Downloading** means fetching the video file as one single, large file using HTTP. Normally this means your user has to download the entire video file before playing it back.

Depending on the size of the file, this might require the user to wait before they can play the video. Therefore, streaming might be more appropriate for bigger files and longer videos. If you don't have access to a streaming server, however, having the file reached via HTTP download might be an easier solution. Additionally, if you know your users have slow Internet connections, or the video needs to be high quality, download could be your best option.

## Progressive Download

Video formats can be optimized for **progressive download**, allowing the video to be playable while the download is in progress. The technical definition of progressive download[63] is that the video is delivered by a regular HTTP web server rather than a streaming server, stored on the viewer's hard drive, and then played from the hard drive.

This is the opposite of streaming, where the video usually is not stored or cached locally, and the viewer can't watch it later. Progressive download is sometimes called "Fast Start".

In addition, HTTP/1.1 allows the browser to request a specific piece of the video resource. You can use the `Accept-Range` HTTP header to tell the server only to deliver a subset of bytes from the total video file, making it more feel like "pseudo streaming[64]". This provides the user with the advantage of not having to wait until the complete file has been downloaded.

# Video Hosting

In order to avoid thinking about what kind of delivery method to use, it might make the most sense to host your video on YouTube or Vimeo—services that are optimized for speedy content delivery.

---

[63] http://www.onlinevideo.net/2011/05/streaming-vs-progressive-download-vs-adaptive-streaming/
[64] http://1stdev.com/tremendum-transcoder/articles/seeking-videos-beyond-the-buffer-line/

In addition, they provide sharing options so you can include your video on your own website. Online video platforms have powerful servers that deliver reliable video content. They normally offer a Flash and HTML5 version of the source as well, making it easily accessible and optimized even on a mobile device.

You could also host the video on your own web server, though some hosting providers limit the amount of bandwidth and data that can be downloaded from your website.

# Web Fonts

You can use custom **web font**s to display fonts that are not installed on the visitor's computer. Using a web font can be especially helpful when a specific font is part of your corporate identity. In Figure 7.4 you can see that airbnb.com makes use of several web fonts:

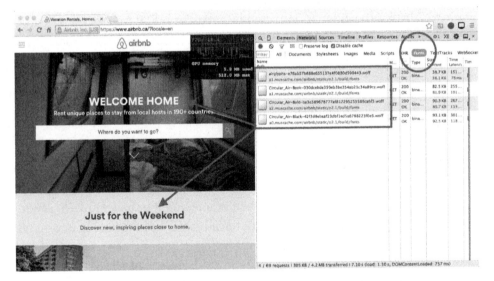

Figure 7.4. *airbnb.com uses several custom fonts, shown via developer tools*

Web fonts have become very popular in recent years. According to HTTP Archive, in October 2014 48%[65] of the top 1 million Alexa websites were using web fonts. However, web fonts come with a performance price. So how do you include web fonts without overly impacting your site's performance?

---

[65] http://httparchive.org/trends.php

You should decide if you want to store the fonts on your server or include them via an external font hosting service. Storing font files on your own server does add to your bandwidth usage, though it saves your browser and extra DNS lookup—which it has to perform when retrieving fonts from a third-party hosting service. However, external hosting services can provide you with optimized solutions to deliver a smooth experience for the user, usually with minimal performance impact.

## Hosting Fonts on Your Own Server

If you want to host a web font on your own server and call it via the standard `@font-face` CSS selector—and have the font rendered by all browsers and platforms—you'll need to make it available in WOFF[66], TTF[67], EOT[68] and SVG[69] formats. In time, it's hoped that WOFF will be supported by all browsers. WOFF is special in that is can be encoded in base64, as a data URI—and as we learned previously, data URI encoding can be beneficial for performance, as it reduces the number of HTTP requests we need to make.

Before adding web fonts to your site, be sure to optimize them. Web fonts vary enormously in size, partly depending on the number of characters they contain. You may only need a few hundred characters, while fonts with comprehensive Unicode coverage can contain thousands of character forms, or **glyphs**. You can actually remove unneeded glyphs from a font file to make it smaller with the help of tools like Glyphs[70] and FontForge[71].

## External Font Hosting

Instead of hosting web fonts on your own server, you can opt for one of the many third-party font services, such as Google Fonts[72] or TypeKit[73]. All you need to do with these services is select a few options to retrieve a simple line of code to include on your site. You do pay a performance price for this, by accepting another DNS lookup; but by choosing a popular web font, you might be able to benefit from **cross-**

---

[66] http://caniuse.com/woff

[67] http://caniuse.com/ttf

[68] http://caniuse.com/eot

[69] http://caniuse.com/svg

[70] http://www.glyphsapp.com/

[71] http://fontforge.github.io

[72] http://www.google.com/fonts

[73] https://typekit.com/

**site caching**. Cross-site caching means that by using a popular, hosted font, the chances are high that your visitor already has the font cached from a previously visited site. It's worth checking out Google Fonts Analytics[74] to find the most popular of its web fonts.

When selecting a Google font, you have the option of defining your character set with a parameter in the API call:

```
<link href="http://fonts.googleapis.com/css?family=Open+Sans&subset=
↪latin" rel="stylesheet">
```

Google Fonts offers a helpful performance gauge for determining the page-load-time impact of including its fonts on your site. In Figure 7.5 you can see that including a relatively simple and limited character set has a small impact, while Figure 7.6 shows that including multiple fonts with multiple sets has a much greater impact:

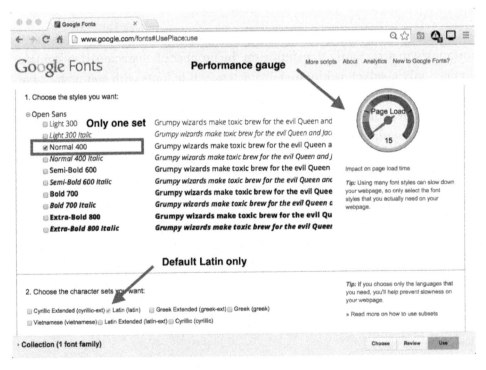

Figure 7.5. Google Fonts service with performance gauge

---

[74] http://www.google.com/fonts#Analytics:total

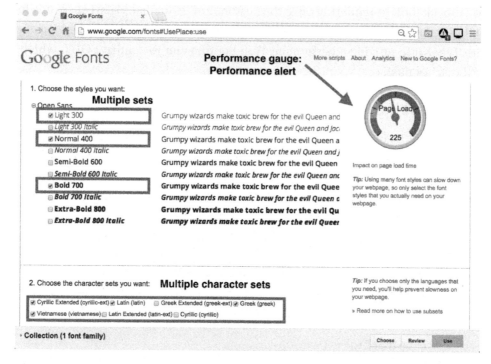

Figure 7.6. Google Fonts service with performance gauge, showing a performance alert

With Google fonts, if you know that you only need one word in a particular web font, you can use the `text` parameter to specify just the characters you need. By using character subsetting, you guarantee the best optimization for the font, as you only request the characters for the specific word:

```
<link href="http://fonts.googleapis.com/css?family=Inconsolata&amp;
➥text=Welcome%20Readers!" rel="stylesheet">
```

Once you've settled on one (or more than one) web font, make sure to asynchronously include it to avoid render blocking.

However, if using asynchronous options, you run into the risk of showing your users a FOUT (flash of unstyled text). Most browsers[75] have adopted FOUT. Chrome and Firefox share the same behaviour when dealing with loading of custom fonts: they timeout after 3 seconds and use a fallback font, and only re-render the text once the font download has completed. IE immediately renders the content with

---

[75] https://www.igvita.com/2014/01/31/optimizing-web-font-rendering-performance

the fallback font, re-rendering once the custom font is loaded. Safari suspends font rendering until the font has completely downloaded. Google has worked together with TypeKit to provide a performant Web Font Loader to combat FOUT, which we'll discuss next.

# Web Font Loader

The Web Font Loader[76] (WFL) provides added control over linked fonts using the `@font-face` attribute. The idea is to help prioritize these assets—for example, by scheduling when to download the font, or how the font should be rendered (synchronously or asynchronously). It fights the FOUT effect by first wrapping the entire HTML content[77] in a `wf-loading` class. The content of `wf-loading` is hidden at first. Once the fonts have loaded, the content visibility is brought back with the `wf-active` class, including a fade-in effect.

The example below shows Open Sans and Satisfy being loaded via WFL:

```
<script>
    WebFontConfig = {
    google: {
       families: ['Open Sans', 'Satisfy']
    }
  };

  (function() {
    var wf = document.createElement('script');
    wf.src = ('https:' == document.location.protocol ? 'https' :
➡ 'http') +
                '://ajax.googleapis.com/ajax/libs/webfont/1.5.6/
➡webfont.js';
    wf.type = 'text/javascript';
    wf.async = 'true';
    var s = document.getElementsByTagName('script')[0];
    s.parentNode.insertBefore(wf, s);
  })();
</script>
```

More information on configuration, and how to include TypeKit fonts, can be found in the WFL documentation.

---

[76] https://github.com/typekit/webfontloader
[77] https://decadecity.net/talks/using-a-web-font-loader

### Font Load Events API

The new Font Load Events API[78]—currently in draft mode—will eventually give full control over managing how and when fonts are loaded and rendered. However, until this API is fully supported in all browsers, I suggest you use WFL.

## Web Font Tips

- Think twice before adding custom fonts, unless they are essential for your company's brand. As well as affecting performance, too many different fonts can clutter your design.

- Consider loading web fonts only on less connection-sensitive devices.

- If you decide to host fonts yourself, optimize them with tools like Glyphs[79] or FontForge[80].

- As a general rule, avoid the hassle of doing it all by yourself. Leverage the power and efforts of Google's font infrastructure, making use of cross-site caching and Google's optimization techniques, thus presenting the user with the most optimized version for their device.

Now that we've discussed ways to optimize our site assets, we'll next look at rolling all these techniques into an automated performance optimization workflow.

## Cool Down

- While images remain the biggest cause of poor web performance, there are many ways to optimize them.

- Select an image format that best suits your purpose, weighing up the advantages and disadvantages of each.

- Use the tools available to you for measuring the performance of each image format, including data URIs.

---

[78] http://dev.w3.org/csswg/css-font-loading/
[79] http://www.glyphsapp.com/
[80] http://fontforge.github.io

- Think carefully about the video format and delivery method you choose—be it streaming, download or progressive download—to help ensure optimal performance.

- Use web fonts wisely, weighing up the needs of design and branding against the performance impact of downloading extra assets. And consider using a web font loader to help you manage font loading during the rendering process.

# Automating Optimization Tasks

## Warm Up

This chapter is my favourite of the entire book. It covers tools that automate website performance optimization. There are innumerable tools for automating the whole gamut of web development tasks, and many of them are well suited to the optimization tasks presented in this book.

In this chapter, I'll first introduce some helpful scripts and APIs that you can use for automation. After explaining how to use these tools, I'll apply them to a concrete example, using the task runner Grunt.

## Automation Tools

This section covers tools for automating performance optimization. Their purpose is to validate code against the performance guidelines discussed in the previous chapters, returning results in a structured format such as JSON or XML.

# PhantomJS in Collaboration with Other Tools

Up until now, we've done all our performance testing manually, so to speak, using tools such as WPT, PageSpeed Insights and the YSlow browser extension. Now we turn instead to PhantomJS[1], a **headless browser**—meaning that you can use it to open a website and run commands on it via the command line. With PhantomJS, we can run the same tests—using YSlow, for example—without ever opening a browser window.

By combining PhantomJS with other tools, you can monitor page and network performance[2], and make this a part of your deployment process.

Here's a simple example of how PhantomJS opens a web page:

```
// open-mypage.js
var page = require('webpage').create();
page.open('http://bbinto.me', function() {
    // do your stuff
    console.log('Just opened bbinto.me');
    phantom.exit();
});
```

You can execute this code as follows:

```
$ phantomjs open-mypage.js
```

Let's look at an actual example of using PhantomJS with YSlow to analyze a simple demo page[3]. Firstly, as a comparison, Figure 8.1 shows the YSlow result in the browser, the site achieving an overall performance score of 87:

---

[1] http://phantomjs.org/

[2] http://phantomjs.org/network-monitoring.html

[3] http://bbinto.me/lean-websites/crp/index.html

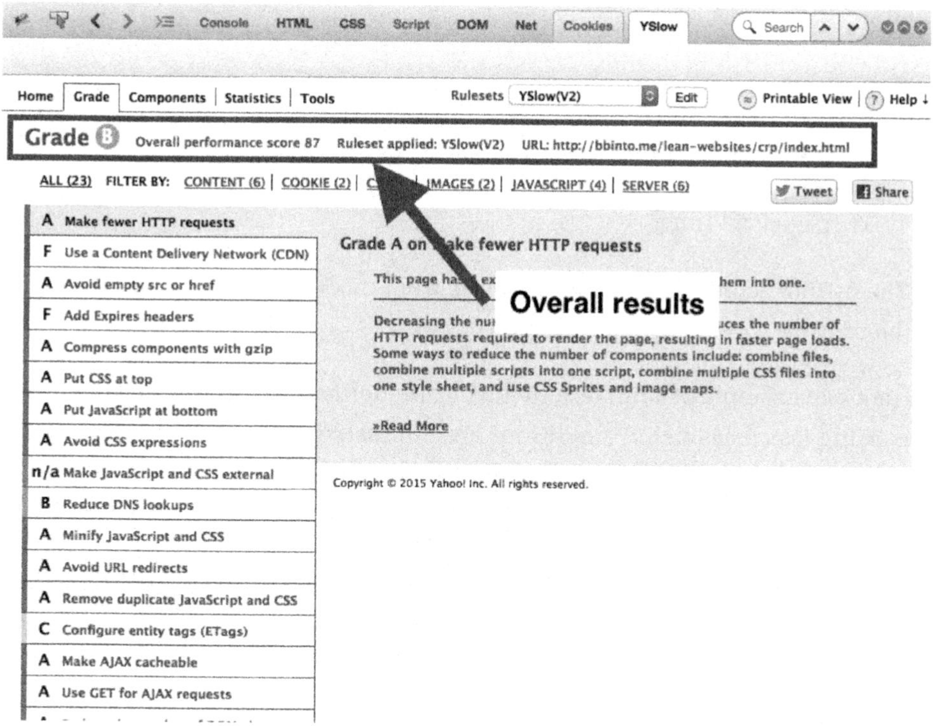

Figure 8.1. YSlow via the Firefox extension, visual representation within browser window

Now let's look at the performance results produced by YSlow via the headless browser.

- Firstly, we retrieve simple JSON output:

```
$ phantomjs yslow.js --info basic http://bbinto.me/lean-websites/
➥crp/index.html

// result
$ {"v":"3.1.8","w":623435,"o":87,"u":"http%3A%2F%2Fbbinto.me%2Fle
➥an-websites%2Fcrp%2Findex.html","r":19,"i":"ydefault","lt":2191}
```

The key to the results is as follows:

- v: version

- w: weight

- o: overall score

- u: URL

- r: number of requests

- i: performance ruleset (from `ydefault`, `yslow1` or `yblog`)

- lt: page load time

The overall score "87" matches the one from the YSlow extension running in the browser.

- Here's an example of a full test, including predefined conditions that the website is being tested against. If conditions are not met, the test fails and returns a warning. The following command defines thresholds to check if the website has an overall score of B (or better):

```
$ phantomjs yslow.js --info basic --format tap --threshold B http:
⇥//bbinto.me/lean-websites/crp/index.html
```

The test passed:

```
$ TAP version 13
1..1
ok 1 B (87) overall score
```

The threshold value can range from 0 to 100 (with 100 being the strictest), or can be validated with A–F marks, where A is the best and F the worst.

You can pick the thresholds appropriate for your website. For example, you could even be more specific and rigorous and set the threshold on HTTP requests (ynumreq:A) to 95, as follows:

```
$ phantomjs yslow.js --info grade --format tap --threshold '{"ynum
⇥req": "95"}' http://bbinto.me/lean-websites/crp/index.html
```

The examples above use the `ydefault` ruleset specified in the **yslow.js** file. That's the same ruleset that is being used when you run YSlow via the browser extension. The ruleset defines how the overall score is calculated, based on the criteria to be tested.

In contrast to using YSlow on its own, using it with PhantomJS allows for more customization of performance tests and thresholds. To make this an even more optimized process, you can add the PhantomJS script to your continuous deployment process. Continuous integration tools such as Jenkins or Travis offer automated testing environments, and can alert you when one of the test criteria fails during website integration or production.

### Continuous Delivery, Continuous Integration

Continuous delivery involves building software such that it can go into production at any time. Continuous integration involves regularly testing and merging changes into a project. Continuous integration builds can be started by various events, such as being triggered by a commit in a version control system, scheduling via a cron-like mechanism, or building when other builds have completed, etc.

Tools such as Jenkins[4] or Travis[5] help organizations to run these processes.

# WPT API and PageSpeed Insights API

Instead of using PhantomJS as your browser to test a website for performance, you can also query performance APIs in the cloud. As noted in Chapter 3, PageSpeed Insights and WPT both offer APIs. You can use these APIs to integrate performance tests into your deployment process.

Let's start with the WPT API, to illustrate how it can be used to detect bad performance decisions without us needing to analyze anything manually in a browser window.

Marcel Duran, a Google Engineer, has built a plugin for the WPT API[6] to work with continuous integration tools.

By providing Duran's WPT API wrapper with a **specs.json** file, you can specify how to run a performance test, and when the test should pass or fail. Let's check out some example content for **specs.json:**

---

[4] http://en.wikipedia.org/wiki/Jenkins_%28software%29
[5] https://travis-ci.org/recent
[6] https://github.com/marcelduran/webpagetest-api/wiki/Test-Specs

```
{
  "median": {
    "firstView": {
      "requests": 20,
      "render": 400,
      "loadTime": 4000
    }
  }
}
```

The sample above creates the following ruleset: the page to be tested should not have more than 20 HTTP requests on first view, the render time should be below 400ms, and the total load time should be less than 4000ms. You're not limited to testing these properties, though. You can use any of the attributes in the WPT API JSON response to define your thresholds.

Here's the command we issue to start the test:

```
webpagetest test http://urltotest.com ---specs specs.json
```

The returning JSON response will be compared with the specs.json file, and outputs the following test result:

```
WebPageTest
    ✓ median.firstView.requests: 10 should be less than 20
    1) median.firstView.render: 600 should be less than 400
    ✓ median.firstView.loadTime: 2500 should be less than 4000
    2) median.firstView.score_gzip: 50 should be greater than 90

  2 passing
  2 failing
```

Similar to YSlow for PhantomJS, you could easily hook into the API from your continuous build machine to monitor your website's performance for each build, issuing an alarm when any threshold has been crossed.

Let's now move on to the PageSpeed Insights API. The following request will provide you with PageSpeed results for bbinto.me:

```
curl GET https://www.googleapis.com/pagespeedonline/v1/runPagespeed?
➥url=http%3A%2F%2Fwww.bbinto.me&key={YOUR_API_KEY}"
```

By default, the result comes back in JSON format, as follows:

```
{
  "kind": "pagespeedonline#result",
  "id": "http://www.bbinto.me/",
  "responseCode": 200,
  "title": "bbinto.me",
  "score": 51,
  "pageStats": {
   "numberResources": 79,
   "numberHosts": 13,
   "totalRequestBytes": "7990",
   "numberStaticResources": 44,
   "htmlResponseBytes": "107091",
   "cssResponseBytes": "249769",
   "imageResponseBytes": "1500676",
   "javascriptResponseBytes": "787229",
   "otherResponseBytes": "115450",
   "numberJsResources": 28,
   "numberCssResources": 10
  },
  // ...
```

Looking at the JSON result above, you could focus on a few criteria, such as the value of `score` or `numberResources`, to trigger an alarm if the defined thresholds have been exceeded. By reading the results of the performance JSON file, you can programmatically detect and react to performance issues without ever having to run the page through the online browser version of PageSpeed Insights.

Note that these validation checks for the PageSpeed API are only possible if your site is already live. If you need to validate results like this before deploying, you will need to look at WPT's private instance[7] and use its API via the private instance. That way, you can test internal integration pages as well. This is especially helpful for newly launching sites.

---

[7] https://sites.google.com/a/webpagetest.org/docs/private-instances

# Task Runners and Build Systems

The goal of task runners is to set up a sequence of tasks that are automatically executed, saving developers from repetitive manual work. There are several popular task runners available, but for the purposes of this book, I will focus on Grunt.

## Grunt

Grunt[8] is a JavaScript-based task runner that not only automates website development and deployment tasks, but also includes handy performance tools. Let's look at a few of them.

| Performance Tools | Description | Applicable Exercise Rule |
|---|---|---|
| grunt-closure-compiler[9] | A Grunt task for Closure Compiler (a tool that minifies and concatenates files). | Reduce file size and HTTP requests |
| grunt-contrib-concat[10] | A Grunt task to combine either JavaScript or CSS files. | Reduce HTTP requests |
| grunt-contrib-cssmin[11] | Once your CSS files are all concatenated, use cssmin to shrink several lines of CSS code into a single line. | Reduce file size |
| grunt-contrib-imagemin[12] | A Grunt task to optimize images used on your page. | Reduce file size |
| grunt-contrib-uglify[13] | Uglify and concat go almost hand in hand and | Reduce file size |

---

[8] http://gruntjs.com/
[9] https://github.com/gmarty/grunt-closure-compiler
[10] https://github.com/gruntjs/grunt-contrib-concat
[11] https://github.com/gruntjs/grunt-contrib-cssmin
[12] https://github.com/gruntjs/grunt-contrib-imagemin
[13] https://github.com/gruntjs/grunt-contrib-uglify

| Performance Tools | Description | Applicable Exercise Rule |
|---|---|---|
|  | should be used together. Concat first combines all defined JavaScript files. Uglify only works on JavaScript files. It minifies all code in a one line block of code. Use cssmin for CSS files. |  |
| grunt-criticalcss[14] | Finds the above the fold CSS for your page, and outputs it into a file. | 14KB head rule |
| grunt-htmltidy[15] | A Grunt task that runs HTML Tidy. | Clean markup |
| grunt-htmlcompressor[16] | A Grunt task to minify and compress HTML files. | Reduce file size |
| grunt-image-embed[17] | This plugin encodes images as base64 and leverages the technique of data URIs for images. | Reduce HTTP requests |
| grunt-montage[18] | A Grunt task to sprite images. ImageMagick is required. | Reduce HTTP requests |
| grunt-pagespeed[19] | A Grunt plugin to run Google PageSpeed Insights as part of CI. | Measure first |

---

[14] https://github.com/filamentgroup/grunt-criticalCSS
[15] https://www.npmjs.org/package/grunt-htmltidy
[16] https://github.com/jney/grunt-htmlcompressor
[17] https://github.com/ehynds/grunt-image-embed
[18] https://github.com/globaldev/grunt-montage
[19] https://www.npmjs.org/package/grunt-pagespeed

| Performance Tools | Description | Applicable Exercise Rule |
|---|---|---|
| grunt-perfbudget[20] | Grunt task for performance budgeting. | Measure first/Setup baseline |
| grunt-phantomas[21] | A Grunt task to produce PhantomJS-based web performance stats collector and monitoring tool. | Measure first |
| grunt-uncss[22] | A Grunt task for removing unused CSS from your projects. | Reducing file size |
| grunt-usemin[23] | A Grunt task that replaces references to non-optimized scripts or style sheets into a set of HTML files. | Reduce HTTP requests |
| SPOFCheck[24] | Can be used via CLI to detect SPOF-potential third-party scripts. | Remove third-party monsters |

Let's take some of the listed tasks above and apply them to an example web page. The page includes a hero image, a link to the jQuery library hosted on Google's CDN, a simple jQuery slideshow with previous and next buttons, and some links to other JavaScript and CSS files. For comparison purposes, I've created two versions of the page, one prior to running Grunt[25] (titled "It's not magic") and the other after running Grunt[26] (titled "It's magic").

Prior to running Grunt, the slideshow images are not optimized, and there are several individual CSS and JavaScript files that aren't minified or concatenated. After

---

[20] https://github.com/tkadlec/grunt-perfbudget
[21] https://www.npmjs.org/package/grunt-phantomas
[22] https://github.com/addyosmani/grunt-uncss
[23] https://github.com/yeoman/grunt-usemin
[24] https://github.com/senthilp/spofcheck
[25] http://bbinto.me/lean-websites/crp-grunt/without/magic.html
[26] http://bbinto.me/lean-websites/crp-grunt/with/magic.html

running Grunt, the page looks the same, but a lot has happened behind the scenes, as I'll detail below.

## Executing Grunt on the Example Page

**Gruntfile.js** defines the tasks to be executed. I've included several performance optimizing tools, such as a SPOF check that assesses any third-party blocking scripts.

The Gruntfile I am using here is a bit too big to list in this book; you can grab a copy of this file from the code archive. To run Grunt, we just execute the `grunt` command on the command line in the folder that contains the project.

So, what has been tested, changed, and improved?

- The local CSS and JavaScript files have been minified and concatenated (using grunt-concat, grunt-uglify, grunt-cssmin).

- The images have been optimized via ImageMagick (using grunt-imagemin).

- The "next" and "previous" buttons have been combined into a single sprite file (using grunt-montage).

- The title has changed from "It's not magic" to "It's magic" (although this isn't really an optimization, using grunt-processhtml).

- The HTML has been compressed, with comments removed (using grunt-html-compressor).

- A test for potential SPOF scripts has been run (using SPOF-check), warning of potential problems during output.

## Comparison

Let's compare the waterfalls for the two versions of the page. The "not magic" version (prior to running Grunt) is shown in Figure 8.2. The "magic" version (after running Grunt) is shown in Figure 8.3. You can see the difference in the number of assets being downloaded:

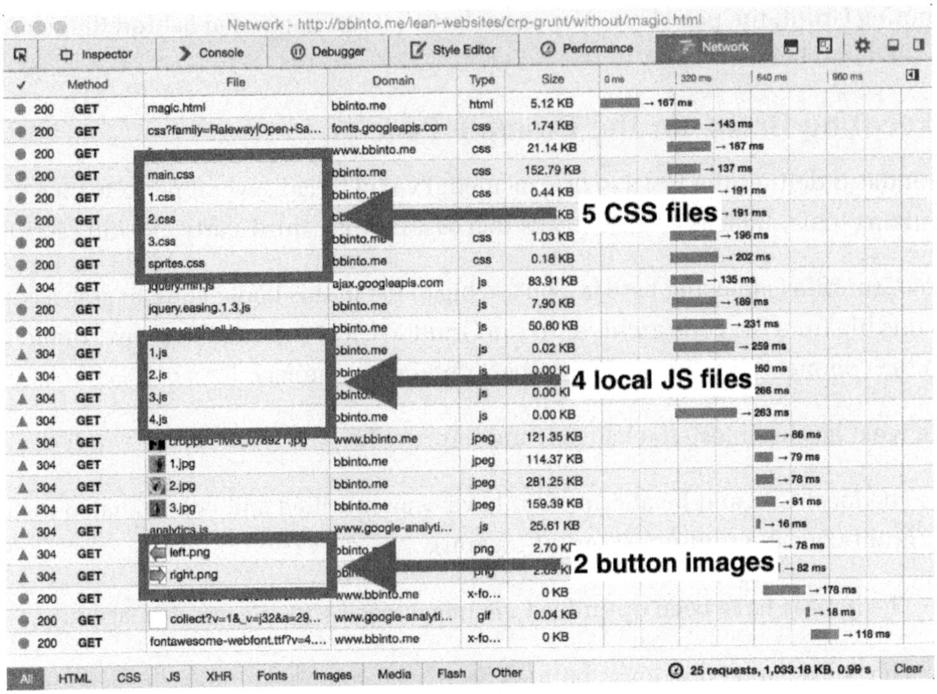

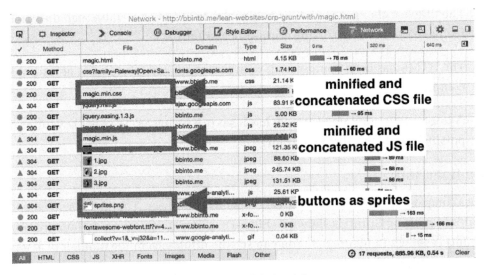

Figure 8.2. Waterfall of the "not magic" page

Figure 8.3. Waterfall of the "magic" page

Let's also have a look at the WPT video comparison of the two pages, specifically focusing on the "Fully Loaded" metric. As you can see, the magic file wins:

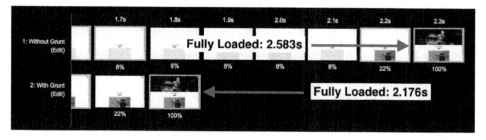

Figure 8.4. WPT video comparison[27] of our pages

Here is the breakdown by WPT metrics:

| Perf Results | Without magic | With magic |
|---|---|---|
| Start Render Time | 1.457s | 1.148s |
| Fully Loaded | 2.583s | 2.176s |
| Bytes | 692KB | 615KB |
| Speed Index | 2222 | 1719 |
| PageSpeed Score | 82 | 88 |

The optimization tasks we've done here with Grunt could have been done manually, but it would be quite a chore to keep working this way on a regular basis. Using task runners to take care of performance optimization can speed up the development process and make producing lean websites easier.

# Grunt Alternatives

Gulp[28] is an alternative to Grunt, similarly automating common performance tasks like minifying JavaScript and compiling preprocessed CSS. While Grunt writes a lot to the file system, changing files, Gulp executes most operations in memory before writing it to disk (using streams). Most of the Grunt tasks are also available for Gulp, such as gulp-concat[29], gulp-minify-html[30], etc.

---

[27] http://www.webpagetest.org/video/compare.php?tests=150123_B7_2RD%2C150123_61_2RB&thumb-Size=100&ival=100&end=visual#

[28] http://gulpjs.com/

[29] https://www.npmjs.com/packages/gulp-concat

[30] https://www.npmjs.com/packages/gulp-minify-html

Other task runners include Maven[31] and Ant[32], which are mainly used for Java projects but can also be used for automated web performance optimization. There are several performance add-ons available, such as Google Closure Compiler[33] or HtmlCompressor[34]. Maven and Ant both use XML to describe the build process.

# Cool Down

▪ You've been setup with tools that can automate your performance optimization tasks.

▪ Most existing performance tools such as YSlow and the WPT API wrapper can be integrated into your continuous deployment process to remove any manual performance testing.

▪ You've been introduced to task runners and build systems, and how they can help you automate performance.

▪ Several specific Grunt performance tools were introduced to demonstrate the benefits of including performance tasks into a deployment process. The comparison of the "before" and "after" pages revealed how many performance improvements can be made without manual labor.

---

[31] http://maven.apache.org/
[32] http://ant.apache.org/
[33] https://github.com/google/closure-compiler
[34] https://code.google.com/p/htmlcompressor/

Chapter

# Network and Server Performance Improvements

## Warm Up

The performance techniques we've covered so far have focused on optimizing the **front-end** of a website—or everything that is downloaded to the browser. In this chapter, we'll focus on improving **back-end** performance, which involves tweaks to your network and web server.

## Content Delivery Networks

A **content delivery network** (CDN) is a hosting service that's optimized for serving content quickly, in an attempt to overcome latency. If a user in Berlin requests a page that is hosted in San Francisco, on a server *without* a CDN, all the assets of that page must be retrieved from San Francisco, making its way over the Atlantic ocean. Pretty cumbersome, don't you think? A CDN alleviates this problem by caching static content at several locations around the globe, allowing site assets to be delivered quickly to any browser.

The following example outlines the performance of a website with and without a CDN:

| velocityconf.com[a] | Original | CDN |
|---|---|---|
| Load Time | 17.87s | 8.34s |
| Start Render | 7.01s | 2.74s |
| Requests | 81 | 81 |
| Bytes in | 1014KB | 792KB |

[a] Source: Sample data for velocityconf.com, taken from Web Performance Today
[http://www.webperformancetoday.com/2012/05/14/cdn-feo-front-end-optimization-web-acceleration/]

The servers available throughout a CDN are called **edge servers**, and distributing multiple copies of a site's content across these servers is called **content replication**. Most CDN providers maintain lots of edge servers around the world, making CDNs particularly useful for sites that serve content to many countries.

Figure 9.1 illustrates how a website is accessed within a CDN. As soon as a page is requested, the optimal server is determined either by the amount of hops needed for the request to reach the server, or by which has the highest availability:

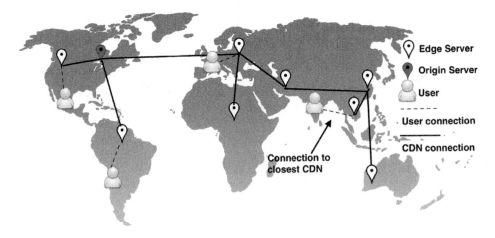

Figure 9.1. Demonstration of a CDN in action

The benefits of using a CDN include:

- **Reduced latency:** by moving the content closer to the user, latency can be reduced and load times improved. Due to content replication and caching of static content at the edge, the user can benefit from cached content and faster delivery times.

- **Reduced packet loss:** because packages travel shorter distances, there's less chance they'll be lost. This is particularly important in latency-sensitive situations, such as video streaming. A poorly streaming video will certainly decrease user satisfaction.

- **Improved reliability:** having content replicated across a CDN improves a website's up-time, as the site isn't dependent on a single server.

# PageSpeed Insights for Your Web Server

PageSpeed Insights is available as a back-end module[1] that can be installed on your server. The module comes with many useful filters[2] that can be installed to optimize your code. The module optimizes the code without requiring you to modify the existing content, executing when the HTTP server delivers the assets. It's basically a performance improvement "on the fly".

The following sections briefly cover a few of the filters that are worth mentioning in the context of reducing HTTP requests, and therefore latency[3].

## Canonicalize JavaScript Libraries

jQuery is one of the most popular JavaScript libraries in use today. Imagine you navigate from website A—which is using jQuery—to website B—which also uses jQuery. The browser automatically fetches the jQuery script again from website B, even though it was just requested from website A.

Something feels inefficient here, doesn't it? It's a waste of bandwidth. So, great minds at Google came up with a solution to reduce this inefficiency by introducing the Canonicalize JavaScript Libraries[4] filter. The idea is that you replace your locally hosted JavaScript libraries (such as jQuery) with the equivalent library hosted on

---

[1] https://developers.google.com/speed/pagespeed/module
[2] https://developers.google.com/speed/pagespeed/module/filters
[3] http://www.modpagespeed.com/ provides a list with before-after samples of applying the mod_pagespeed filters.
[4] https://developers.google.com/speed/pagespeed/module/filter-canonicalize-js

Google's CDN—which means that when browsing, users can utilize a copy of jQuery that was previously fetched from Google's CDN (and which was thus cached in the browser).

Enable the filter as follows (for Apache):

```
ModPagespeedEnableFilters canonicalize_javascript_libraries
```

And here is an example of how the module would replace the local jQuery file as shown below:

```
<html>
  <head>
    <script src="/local/jquery-1.8.3.js">
    </script>
    <script src="foo.js">
    </script>
    <script src="bar.js">
    </script>
  </head>
  <body>
  <!-- fun stuff -->
  </body>
</html>
```

will be rewritten to

```
<html>
  <head>
    <script src="http://ajax.googleapis.com/ajax/libs/jquery/1.8.3/
➥jquery.min.js">
    </script>
    <script src="foo.js">
    </script>
    <script src="bar.js">
    </script>
  </head>
  <body>
```

```
<!-- fun stuff -->
</body>
</html>
```

 **Watch Out For Potential SPOF**

Watch out for synchronous script blockers when using the `canonicalize_javas-cript_libraries` filter. The filter will replace your local version with a third-party version of the script. If you haven't included the script asynchronously, and the third-party provider goes down unexpectedly, this could potentially cause SPOF.

# Combine CSS

The Combine CSS[5] filter looks for all CSS `link` tags on the page. The module removes all individual CSS link tags and concatenates the CSS files into one merged file, which it places wherever the first CSS `link` originally was. This is similar to the concatenating technique we saw previously.

You can enable this via your Apache web server as follows:

```
ModPagespeedEnableFilters combine_css
```

As an example, imagine this as the original HTML:

```
<html>
  <head>
    <link rel="stylesheet" type="text/css" href="styles/1.css">
    <link rel="stylesheet" type="text/css" href="styles/2.css">
    <link rel="stylesheet" type="text/css" href="styles/3.css">
  </head>
  <body>
    <!-- fun stuff -->
  </body>
</html>
```

Combine CSS would turn it into something like this:

---

[5] https://developers.google.com/speed/pagespeed/module/filter-css-combine

```
<html>
  <head>
    <link rel="stylesheet" type="text/css" href="styles/1.css+2.css+
➥3.css.pagespeed.cc.yu2He3_gBx.css">
  </head>
  <body>
    <!-- fun stuff -->
  </body>
</html>
```

# Defer JavaScript

The Defer JavaScript[6] filter follows the `defer` attribute logic that we discussed in Chapter 6. The `defer` attribute delays the JavaScript execution of the script until after the DOM has finished loading. The script with a `defer` attribute attached to it is added to the end of the list of scripts. To ensure that the script can be safely executed at the end of the page load, the attribute should only be used on scripts that don't modify the DOM. The performance advantage comes from stopping scripts blocking other processes in the browser.

The Defer JavaScript filter automatically adds the `src` attribute to any `script` tag on the page. A `window.onload` handler is added to the HTML that then executes all the deferred scripts.

Include this line in your web server config file (for Apache):

```
ModPagespeedEnableFilters defer_javascript
```

If you don't want a script to have the `defer` attribute added—for example, because the script alters the DOM—just add the `pagespeed_no_defer` attribute:

```
<script pagespeed_no_defer="" src="execute.js"></script>
```

In order to demonstrate this, it's best to actually view it in the browser. Check out the before[7] and after[8] pages to view the impact of this filter.

---

[6] https://developers.google.com/speed/pagespeed/module/filter-js-defer
[7] http://www.modpagespeed.com/defer_javascript.html?ModPagespeed=off
[8] http://www.modpagespeed.com/defer_javascript.html?ModPagespeed=on&ModPagespeedFilters=defer_javascript

# Prioritize Critical CSS

The Prioritize Critical CSS[9] filter parses the CSS file and replaces it with just rules used on that page. This aligns with the critical rendering path paradigm, which is to serve the ATF CSS as soon as possible to improve the initial render time.

Include the following line in your web server config file:

```
ModPagespeedEnableFilters prioritize_critical_css
```

The following page includes an external **style.css** file where only the class="red" is being referenced on that page:

```
<html>
  <head>
    <link rel="stylesheet" href="style.css">

    <!-- content of style.css
         .red {color: red;}
         .big { font-size: 8em; }
         .gallery {border:1p solid black; }
    -->
  </head>
  <body>
    <div class="red">
      Hello readers!
    </div>
  </body>
</html>
```

The filter will output as follows, only focusing on the style that is really being used on this page:

```
<html>
  <head>
    <style>
      .red{red;}
    </style>
    </head>
  <body>
```

---

[9] https://developers.google.com/speed/pagespeed/module/filter-prioritize-critical-css

```
    <div class="red">
      Hello readers!
    </div>
  </body>
</html>
<noscript><link rel="stylesheet" href="style.css"></noscript>
```

# Keep-alive

As discussed in Chapter 3, every time an HTTP client—such as a browser—fetches a website asset, it will create a new TCP session to the server, initiating a handshake between the client and the server. After the asset has been received, the server will close the TCP session again to free up resources. If another asset needs to be fetched, the browser again opens another TCP session to the same server. This is inefficient, especially for web pages with a large number of elements, or if the user has a slow network connection—since repeatedly creating and closing TCP connections (one for each message) is like hanging up and redialing the phone[10] between each exchange in a conversation.

HTTP **keep-alive**[11] is intended to solve this problem, by keeping the TCP connection open between the client and the server once the HTTP transaction has completed. If the browser requests another asset from the server, a new TCP session doesn't have to be created.

Without keep-alive, each request will incur two roundtrips[12] of latency. In HTTP/1.1, keep-alive is enabled by default. For HTTP/1.0, you'll need to set it via the `Connection: keep-alive` header. You can either do this via the **.htaccess** file, or by updating your web server configuration file:

```
<!-- your .htaccess file -->
<ifModule mod_headers.c> Header set Connection keep-alive </ifModule>
```

You can verify if keep-alive is enabled for a page by checking out the request header via the developer tools, as shown in Figure 9.2:

---

[10] http://nginx.com/blog/http-keepalives-and-web-performance/
[11] http://en.wikipedia.org/wiki/HTTP_persistent_connection
[12] http://chimera.labs.oreilly.com/books/1230000000545/ch11.html

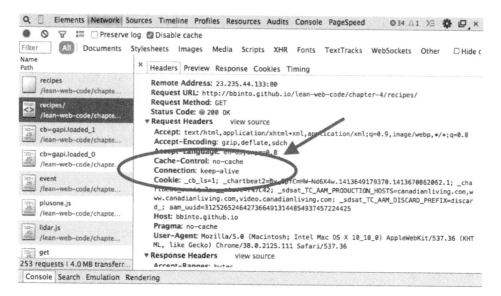

Figure 9.2. Verifying keep-alive in Chrome developer tools

# HTTP/2

As of February 2015, the HTTP/2 specification has been approved[13] by the Internet Engineering Task Force (IETF)[14].

When HTTP/1.1 was introduced a decade ago, latency wasn't something that was worried about. However, times, technologies, and user expectations have changed. HTTP/1.1 is not enough to cope with today's challenges. Today's user demands speedy and instant delivery of content, across different devices, and in different locations, causing higher delays and requiring better handling of HTTP requests. These performance issues have finally been addressed with HTTP/2.

In HTTP/1.1, only the client can initiate a request. Even if the server knows the client needs a resource, it has no mechanism to inform the client and must instead wait to receive a request for the resource from the client. HTTP/2.0 promises to make HTTP requests more efficient[15], reducing the need for workaround techniques to minimize HTTP requests, and thus reducing latency.

---

[13] http://www.ietf.org/blog/2015/02/http2-approved/

[14] IETF is an open, international community of network designers, operators, vendors, and researchers concerned with the evolution of the Internet architecture and the smooth operation of the Internet. The goal of the IETF is to make the Internet work better.

[15] https://www.mnot.net/blog/2014/01/30/http2_expectations

One of the main advantages of HTTP/2 over HTTP/1.1 is that it allows many concurrent HTTP requests to run across one single TCP connection. Without a persistent connection (using keep-alive), the handshake, as discussed in chapter 3, is enforced by HTTP/1.1, causing latency and delays. While the idea of keep-alive is to keep the TCP connection open, HTTP/2 delivers even more improvements. It comes with default HTTP header compression, as opposed to HTTP/1.1, which uses optional compression. In addition, with HTTP/2, the server can proactively send the client the resource it will need, known as **server push**.

Although HTTP/2 is a significant improvement, be aware that using HTTP/2 in the near future will still require you to do your homework. This protocol won't magically remove render blocking and synchronous third-party scripts, or minify scripts for you. These techniques will still have to be employed to make this new protocol shine.

However, with HTTP/2, many small assets can be multiplexed in parallel, and techniques such as resource bundling—image spriting and concatenation—aren't necessary anymore[16] to improve performance.

 ### What About SPDY?

SPDY[17] (pronounced SPeeDY) was introduced prior to HTTP/2, and was a big motivation for most of the features for HTTP/2—and is therefore often considered to be its predecessor. In February 2015, SPDY's inventor, Google, officially said goodbye to SPDY[18] and welcomed HTTP/2 into the world.

# Gzip Compression

Gzip is a very efficient compression program that can easily be enabled on your server to shave off some milliseconds from your page load time. Your server will use Gzip to compress files before sending them to your users. I highly recommend you enable Gzip compression on your server, as it's a very quick and easy performance win.

---

[16] http://chimera.labs.oreilly.com/books/1230000000545/ch13.html#_removing_1_x_optimizations
[17] http://www.chromium.org/spdy/spdy-whitepaper
[18] http://blog.chromium.org/2015/02/hello-http2-goodbye-spdy-http-is_9.html

## When to Use Gzip

Gzip makes most sense for uncompressed, text-based formats such as HTML, XML, JSON and CSS files. Content types that have already been compressed (PDF and images), should not be gzipped, as their file size could actually be increased[19].

But how do you know that Gzip is enabled? You can either open the developer tools of your browser and check the response headers, as shown in Figure 9.3, or use tools such as the HTTP compression test[20], as shown in Figure 9.4:

Figure 9.3. Checking the main HTML page response headers in Firefox's developer tools

---

[19] https://developer.yahoo.com/performance/rules.html#gzip
[20] http://checkgzipcompression.com

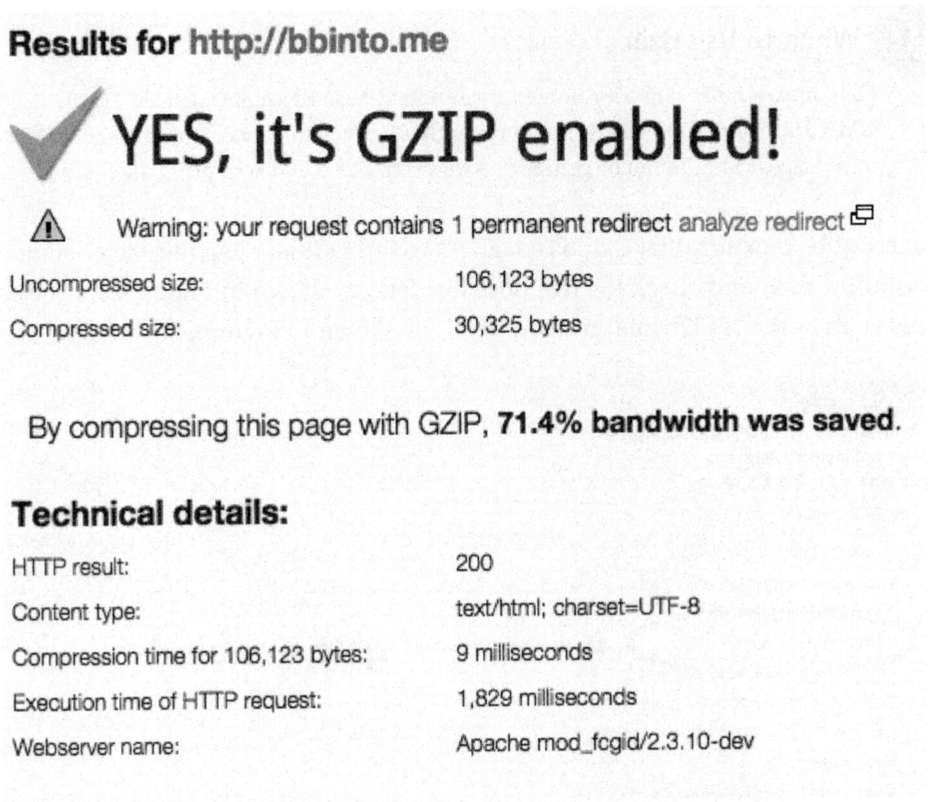

**Results for http://bbinto.me**

✓ YES, it's GZIP enabled!

⚠ Warning: your request contains 1 permanent redirect analyze redirect ⊡

Uncompressed size:                                106,123 bytes

Compressed size:                                   30,325 bytes

By compressing this page with GZIP, **71.4% bandwidth was saved**.

**Technical details:**

HTTP result:                                        200

Content type:                                       text/html; charset=UTF-8

Compression time for 106,123 bytes:                 9 milliseconds

Execution time of HTTP request:                     1,829 milliseconds

Webserver name:                                     Apache mod_fcgid/2.3.10-dev

Figure 9.4. Using HTTP compression test to check Gzip compression status

All modern browsers support Gzip compression, so we just need to make sure that it's enabled in the web server configuration file. Some web servers already have Gzip enabled. HTML5 Boilerplate gives detailed instructions[21] on how to enable Gzip for most common web servers.

If you don't own your web server, you can enable Gzip via the **.htaccess** file for Apache servers, or other equivalent files for different web servers (such as **web.config** for IIS).

Let's look at how to enable it on Apache:

```
<ifModule mod_gzip.c>
    mod_gzip_on Yes
    mod_gzip_dechunk Yes
```

---

[21] https://github.com/h5bp/server-configs

```
    mod_gzip_item_include file .(html?|txt|css|js|php|pl)$
    mod_gzip_item_include handler ^cgi-script$
    mod_gzip_item_include mime ^application/x-javascript.*
    mod_gzip_item_exclude mime ^image/.*
    mod_gzip_item_exclude rspheader ^Content-Encoding:.*gzip.*
</ifModule>
```

If you want to compare the performance of your site gzipped and not gzipped, you can set the following line in your Apache `.htaccess` file to disable Gzip:

```
SetEnv gzip 1
```

Figure 9.5 shows WPT results for my website, with and without Gzip enabled:

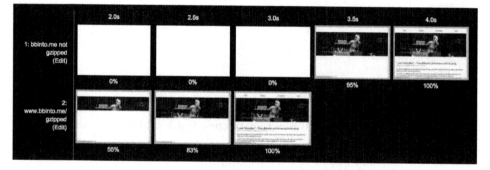

Figure 9.5. *WPT comparison*[22] *of bbinto.me without and with Gzip enabled*

You can see a clear difference in performance between the gzipped and non-gzipped versions. My gzipped site loaded almost one second faster. My speed index improved from 3140 to 2100, and my start to render time improved from 3.05s to 1.94s. Gzip can be a simple and quick performance win.

# Caching

We briefly talked about caching in Chapter 5, but let's dig deeper into this topic, as caching can be a real performance enhancer.

Before going into more detail on how caching can improve performance, let's first take a look at how we can get more information about assets and their current caching policy.

---

[22] http://www.webpagetest.org/video/compare.php?tests=141011_G7_JD1,141011_7E_K5J

In Figure 9.6, you can see that when I visit google.ca, some of the images my browser is fetching come from the browser cache for Google's search landing page. That's not a surprise, because I use Google several time throughout the day:

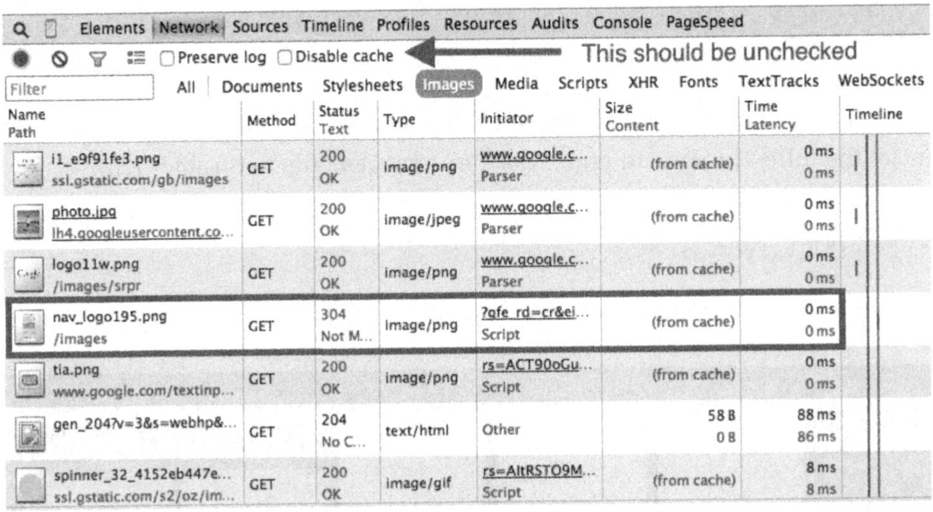

Figure 9.6. Using developer tools to assess caching on google.ca

Looking closer, you can see that **nav_logo195.png** is a sprite image, as shown in Figure 9.7. It makes sense for Google to set a very long cache time for this particular image, as the logo shouldn't change that often:

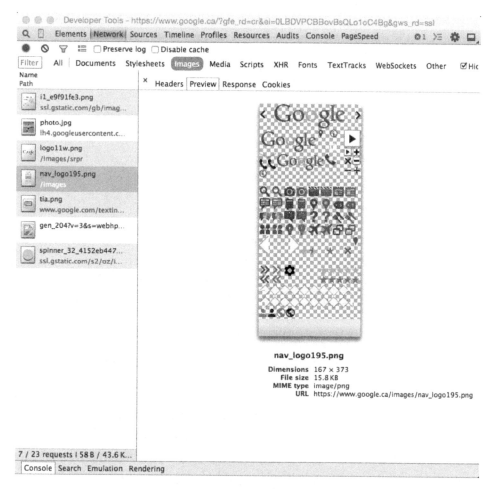

Figure 9.7. A sprite image on google.ca

Now, let's move on to discuss how we can improve performance through caching. The basic idea is to avoid as many unnecessary HTTP requests as possible, by storing certain assets in the browser that can be reused. Every browser includes a cache, but needs to get instructions on how and when to use it. You can set that logic, such as when to request a newer, or fresher version of an asset, and when not to use the version in the cache, by using the Cache-Control header.

To illustrate the use of caching headers, let's take a look at the response headers from the previous Google sprite image, as outlined in the red box in Figure 9.8. The response header is sent by the server, while the request header is sent by a browser to a server:

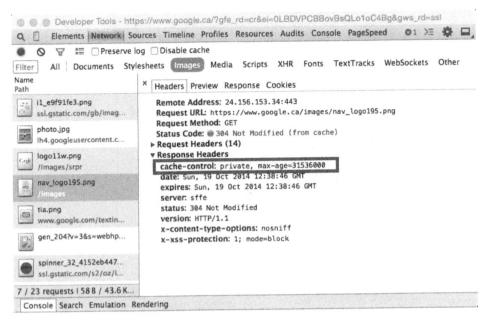

Figure 9.8. Checking out Cache-Control headers for the sprite image

Let's have a look at the `Cache-Control` header. Its settings are called **cache response directives**. The first directive is either `public`, `private`, `max-age`, or `no-cache`.

- **public**: a public, or "shared" cache is leveraged by more than one client. Because of that, it provides great performance gain, because a user may receive a cached copy from somebody else without ever having to obtain the original copy from the origin. Publicly cacheable assets could be logos, navigation items, JavaScript and CSS files etc.—anything that is requested very frequently by most or every visitor to your site.

- **private**: a private cache is only used by a single client and not shared. It allows caching of assets that are specific to one user in a browser. No proxy server will cache the response. This is mostly used when people access assets that need authorization and are served via HTTPS. The Google image example above uses a private directive, so the asset can't be picked up by intermediate caches[23] or CDNs to be used for other users to retrieve.

---

[23] Intermediate caches are caches between the edge and the user, such as corporations and schools that have a cache in their network.

- **max-age=[seconds]**: specifies the maximum amount of time in seconds that the asset is considered fresh. This directive is relative to the time of the request. In the Google image example, the max-age is set to 31536000 seconds, or 365 days. These Cache-Control directives leave the asset in the browser cache for 365 days before checking if a newer version is available to fetch.

- **no-cache**: every time the asset is requested, the cache needs to submit a request to the origin for confirmation before releasing a cached copy.

More on the different directives can be found in the W3C Header Field Definitions document[24].

# Conditional Requests

Besides the caching directives set in the Cache-Control header, there are additional headers you can use to check for specific conditions of the asset; and these conditions can be used to determine if an updated copy of the asset should be fetched. These conditional requests can be content-based (ETag) or time-based (If-modified-since) states, or states that improve performance while the updated version of the asset is being fetched (stale-while-revalidate, stale-if-error).

## Content-based

You will notice that some assets also have an ETag in the response header. When a browser is directed by a Cache-Control setting to refresh an asset, but the asset hasn't changed, that's where the ETag comes in. The ETag is generated by the server, and is an arbitrary token (such as an MD5 hash) that acts as a fingerprint of the contents of the asset. If the hash is still the same as the value of If-None-Match in the request header, then the browser knows the asset hasn't changed, and so skips the download. Find more information on how to create ETags from Yahoo's Best Practices for Speeding Up Your Web Site[25].

Here's an example of an ETag in use. The following snippet is an HTTP request header if-None-Match, and the corresponding response header with the ETag hash for a style sheet on my website **/css/services.css**. The hash is the same, indicating that the content of the style sheet hasn't changed from the version in the cache, so the content doesn't need to be downloaded again.

---

[24] http://www.w3.org/Protocols/rfc2616/rfc2616-sec14.html#sec14.9
[25] https://developer.yahoo.com/performance/rules.html#etags

▦ Request header:

```
GET /css/services.css?ver=2015Febaa HTTP/1.1
...
If-None-Match: "532a0d9b-bd8+gzip"
...
```

▦ Response header:

```
HTTP/1.1 304 Not Modified
...
Etag: "532a0d9b-bd8+gzip"
...
```

## Time-based

Conditional time-based headers[26], such as `If-modified-since` (in the request header) and `Last-modified` (in the response header), can be set to only request a fresh version of the asset if it actually has been modified since the browser's copy was cached. If the cached copy is the most up-to-date, then the server will not serve any new copy and returns a 304 (not modified) response code.

The following snippet is an HTTP request header of `if-modified-since`, and its corresponding response header with the `Last-modified` response for a style sheet on my website **/css/services.css**.

▦ Request header:

```
GET /css/services.css?ver=2015Febaa HTTP/1.1
...
If-Modified-Since: Wed, 19 Mar 2014 21:35:23 GMT
...
```

▦ Response header:

---

[26] https://devcenter.heroku.com/articles/increasing-application-performance-with-http-cache-headers

```
HTTP/1.1 304 Not Modified
...
Last-Modified: Wed, 19 Mar 2014 21:35:23 GMT
...
```

The `Last-modified` date is not newer than the `If-Modified-Since` date, and therefore no new copy has to be requested.

## stale-while-revalidate

**Stale** content[27] describes an older version of the asset that the browser keeps using from the cache. The `stale-*` extensions allow the browser to continue using stale content under specific conditions, while it's trying to retrieve a newer copy of the asset from the server in the background.

The `stale-while-revalidate` header allows the browser to keep using the current, possibly stale, version of the asset, until the amount of time you specify in the header. In the meantime, the newest version of the asset is being re-fetched in the background. By updating the asset in the background, we achieve optimal utilization of the cache:

```
HTTP/1.1 200 OK
Cache-Control: max-age=86400, stale-while-revalidate=43200
Content-Type: text/plain
```

The asset will be read from the cache for 86400 seconds (1 day). After that time has passed, the cache will re-fetch the requested asset. If we didn't set `stale-while-revalidate`, the page would load more slowly. Instead, we give the cache up to 43200 seconds (half a day) to re-fetch the new version in the background, thus ensuring fast-loading assets for the end user.

## stale-if-error

When the `stale-if-error` header is set, it allows the user to receive the asset from the CDN without interruption, even if there is an issue with the asset at the origin server. Instead of showing a broken asset, it will instead serve the stale content to improve availability:

---

[27] http://tools.ietf.org/html/rfc5861

```
HTTP/1.1 200 OK
Cache-Control: max-age=1000, stale-if-error=1200
Content-Type: text/plain
```

In the example above, the response first indicates that the asset will be fresh for 1000 seconds. In addition, the asset can be used for another 1200 seconds. If an error occurs after that, it becomes stale.

Not many websites are utilizing these optimization features yet. As of January 2015[28], 0.2% of the top Alexa websites use `stale-while-revalidate` for their assets, and only 0.1% use `stale-if-error`.

# Caching in Practice

In order to benefit from the caching options mentioned above, the caching headers need to be set in your web server configuration file. We normally refer to this set up as the caching *policy*.

It's good practice for every developer to lay out a set of carefully formulated `Cache-Control` policies, outlining the website's assets according to their expected lifetimes.

Structuring your website into logical directories can be very beneficial when creating a caching policy. Review your assets and split them into multiple directories based on their nature. For example, branding and logo files that rarely change could be stored in a folder of assets to be cached for a long time, while dynamic content could be stored in a separate folder with a short cache time.

Let's take a look at an example. My website is a WordPress blog, and I don't intend to change the design of it that often. So setting a longer time in the cache for my theme files makes perfect sense. Furthermore, I try to update my website with a new blog post every two to three months, depending on my schedule. So I want to make sure that I'm taking this writing schedule into consideration when setting the cache policy for the HTML files. To be on the safe side, let's set it to one month. I also decided to set a cache value of one year for all my uploads, such as images, PDFs, and text files, assuming they rarely change once I've uploaded them.

---

[28] http://bbinto.github.io/lean-web-code/chapter-9/cache-headers-stale-jan2015.xlsx

Since I have different expiration times for each of those folders, I'll need to create a separate **.htaccess** file for each folder.

Let's update the **.htaccess** files according to my proposed caching goals.

▨ **/var/www/htdocs/bbinto.me/.htaccess:**

```
<ifModule mod_headers.c>
    ExpiresActive On
    # Expires after 1 month
    <filesMatch ".(html)$">
    Header set Cache-Control "max-age=2592000"
    </filesMatch>
</ifModule>
```

▨ **/var/www/htdocs/bbinto.me/wp-content/themes/matheson/.htaccess:**

```
<ifModule mod_headers.c>
    ExpiresActive On
    # Expires after 6 months
    Header set Cache-Control "max-age=15552000"
</ifModule>
```

▨ **/var/www/htdocs/bbinto.me/wp-content/uploads/.htaccess:**

```
<ifModule mod_headers.c>
    ExpiresActive On
    # Expires after 1 year
    Header set Cache-Control "max-age=31104000"
</ifModule>
```

If you have direct access to your web server's config file (on Apache, it would be httpd.conf), you can use <Directory> to define all folders in one config file instead of putting separate **.htaccess** files into each directory individually:

```
# Expires after 6 months
<Directory "/var/www/htdocs/bbinto.me/wp-content/themes/matheson">
    Header set Cache-Control "max-age=15552000"
</Directory>
```

```
# Expires after 1 month
<filesMatch ".(html)$">
Header set Cache-Control "max-age=2592000"
</filesMatch>

# Expires after 1 year
<Directory "/var/www/htdocs/bbinto.me/wp-content/uploads/">
    Header set Cache-Control "max-age=31104000"
</Directory>
```

As shown above, I applied some simple rules to files and folders, but you could also include regular expressions to include or exclude certain content types or directories.

After I finished setting up my caching policy, I ran my site through WPT without[29] and with[30] the cache policy in place. For this example, I only compared the **Repeat** view results, as that will reflect use of the cache settings.

|  | **Without cache** | **With cache** | **Savings** |
|---|---|---|---|
| **Load Time** | 6.629s | 2.485s | 62% |
| **Start Render** | 3.108s | 1.120s | 63% |
| **Speed Index** | 4296 | 1108 | 74% |

As you can see, using the cache can make a significant difference to the performance of the page. Google has a useful decision tree[31] to help you decide how to set up efficient caching policies.

### Using Developer Tools to Check Caching

The developer tools in your browser normally have a check box that you can enable or disable to see how the website loads with and without the cache set[32].

---

[29] http://www.webpagetest.org/result/141019_C0_MWG/1/details/cached/
[30] http://www.webpagetest.org/result/141019_TB_MY7/1/details/cached/
[31] https://developers.google.com/web/fundamentals/performance/optimizing-content-efficiency/http-caching?hl=en#defining-optimal-cache-control-policy
[32] http://devtoolsecrets.com/secret/performance-disable-the-browser-cache.html

You can either find the option under the **Network** tab (Chrome), under **Settings** (Firefox), or under the **Developer tools** menu (Safari).

# Caching Tips

It's worth noting that there is no caching silver bullet that you can apply to all the assets of your site. Take your time auditing and defining your resources and their optimal cache lifetime. Each asset will have different "freshness" requirements. Here are a few tips[33] to get you started thinking:

▦ For static assets, or assets that rarely change, Google suggests setting an expiration policy of one year[34], or minimum of one week. For example, there's no need to re-fetch an asset if it rarely changes, such as a logo.

▦ Use consistent URLs—don;t serve the same content through different URLs. additionally, pay attention to how they are typed in. As URLs are case sensitive, the same page could be cached multiple times unnecessarily.

▦ Define a cache policy for your assets: differentiate between often changing assets vs. very static assets that rarely change. Audit and determine the appropriate `max-age` for these assets.

▦ If you use a CDN, identify the assets that are identical for all your users. These are good candidates for CDN caching.

▦ As mentioned before, think before you concatenate. For example, before merging all your JavaScript files into one, evaluate if there might be a piece of your web application that changes more frequently, and consequently the corresponding JavaScript code that comes with it. Separate this file with a less aggressive cache policy.

# Cool Down

▦ You've learned how a CDN works and how it can reduce latency.

---

[33] https://developers.google.com/web/fundamentals/performance/optimizing-content-efficiency/http-caching#caching-checklist

[34] https://developers.google.com/speed/docs/insights/LeverageBrowserCaching

▓ You've been introduced to the PageSpeed Insights web server module, which includes several useful performance-enhancing filters, such as `canonic-alize_javascript_libraries` and `combine_css`.

▓ You've learned about the challenges for HTTP/1.1 in keeping up with today's web demands, and that HTTP/2 has been introduced to address these issues—including latency, which is one of the biggest challenges for the web.

▓ You've learned how you can gain great performance improvements with some simple adjustments to your web server setup, such as gzipping and using `keep-alive`.

▓ You've been introduced to caching policies and how to set them up.

# A Multi-device Web World

## Warm Up

We've covered lots of ways to optimize site performance, but we still need to discuss how to serve the right content to users based on their device and the circumstances they're in. Getting this right can also result in significant performance improvements.

Detecting devices is a crucial part of this. In this chapter, we'll look at how to identify if your users are on a laptop, tablet or smartphone, and if they're on a fast or slow connection. We'll also look at why performance on mobile devices is especially important.

## One Web in a Multi-device World

One Web means making, as far as is reasonable, the same information and services available to users irrespective of the device they are using. However, it does not mean that exactly the same information is available in exactly the same representation across all devices. The context of mobile use, device capability variations, bandwidth issues and mobile network capabilities all affect the representation. (W3C Mobile Web Best Practices[1])

This quote, from the W3C Mobile Web Initiative's Best Practices Working Group, summarizes how we should build websites for multiple devices. Different devices with different capabilities and screen sizes require us to build websites targeted to each device if we want to provide the best user experience.

It doesn't always make sense to serve exactly the same content to all users. Imagine a glossy, image-heavy travel website. That might be a nice experience for a desktop user on a broadband connection, but terrible for a user on a small mobile device. The images most likely should be reduced in size for faster download and to save bandwidth—if they even need to be displayed at all. It may also be that the mobile user just wants to check itinerary details or departure times, so the layout and functionality appropriate for the desktop may be quite inappropriate in the mobile context. Providing users with the best experience to help them accomplish their goal should be the main focus.

# Mobile on the Rise: Current Stats and Internet Usage

In the early days of the web, we could be pretty certain that our site visitors were on a wired Internet connection with only a few browsers to choose from. Nowadays, there's a lot more fragmentation across a multitude of devices, browsers and types of Internet connections—which makes it more important to consider how best to serve web content.

StatCounter[2] provides useful data on the most commonly used screen sizes, operating systems and so forth. Based on the StatCounter top lists (at the time of writing), there are approximately 14[3] different screen resolutions, 8[4] operating systems, 9[5] browsers, many different connection speeds, and around 14,000 different user agent strings (device types) worldwide.

---

[1] http://www.w3.org/TR/mobile-bp/#OneWeb
[2] http://gs.statcounter.com
[3] http://gs.statcounter.com/#all-resolution-ww-yearly-2012-2014
[4] http://gs.statcounter.com/#all-os-ww-yearly-2012-2014
[5] http://gs.statcounter.com/#all-browser-ww-yearly-2012-2014

The steep rise in mobile usage looks like it will continue. In 2014, there were around 7.2 billion[6] people in the world, with around 4.55 billion mobile users[7] worldwide. Based on predictions[8] for 2015, the worldwide population is expected to reach 7.4 billion, while the number of mobile phone subscriptions is calculated to be marginally over 7.5 billion.

In addition, there are suggestions[9] that mobile browsing will surpass desktop browsing, and that in some areas it might already have done so. That's reason enough to ensure our sites are *performance bulletproof* on mobile devices.

# Mobile Performance Challenges

This section looks at current mobile constraints, and why a lean website for mobile users is especially important.

## Speed

First off, how much slower is mobile? Akamai's *State of the Internet Report from Q2, 2014*[10] collected "real" page load times from around the world via RUM. (Note that this RUM data only includes devices with Navigation Timing API support.) The results vary greatly from country to country and across continents.

Akamai defines the difference between page load time on mobile vs. non-mobile as the "mobile penalty". Here is some of the data collected, with the highest penalty country at the top and the lowest at the bottom:

| Country | Avg. PLT on Broadband (ms) | Avg. PLT on Mobile (ms) | Mobile Penalty |
|---------|----------------------------|-------------------------|----------------|
| Ireland | 1508 | 5353 | 3.6x |
| Canada | 3014 | 5321 | 1.8x |
| United States | 3354 | 5299 | 1.6x |

---

[6] http://www.worldometers.info/world-population/
[7] http://www.emarketer.com/Article/Smartphone-Users-Worldwide-Will-Total-175-Billion-2014/1010536
[8] http://www.icinsights.com/news/bulletins/Worldwide-Cellphone-Subscriptions-Forecast-To-Exceed-Worldwide-Population-In-2015/
[9] http://telecoms.com/301771/half-of-worlds-population-on-mobile-web-by-2020-report/
[10] http://www.akamai.com/html/about/press/releases/2014/press-093014.html

| Country | Avg. PLT on Broadband (ms) | Avg. PLT on Mobile (ms) | Mobile Penalty |
|---------|----------------------------|-------------------------|----------------|
| Turkey  | 3320                       | 2335                    | 0.7x           |

Why is everything so much slower on mobile? There are several performance constraints to consider when developing websites for mobile devices. Let's go through them.

## Mobile Network and High Latency

Wireless communication comes with more latency than wired communication. Wireless connections are based on the radio in the device, and need to travel through the air, exposed to a lot of congestion and interference. Hence, there's more latency involved in requesting a website on a mobile connection than from a LAN or even WiFi connection at home. Let me explain why, by going through high-level, simplified steps on how a mobile device requests a web page. (Ilya Grigorik has a very detailed chapter[11] on this in his *High Performance Browser Networking* book.)

1. Initially, the radio is off, and the phone is in an idle state.

2. As soon as you type a URL into the browser, the radio tries to establish a connection with a nearby radio tower. While traveling over air to the nearest radio tower, the request is exposed to interference. This is the addition of unwanted signals to a useful signal, such as electromagnetic interference[12], co-channel interference[13], or inter-carrier interference[14]. This step of negotiating the radio link can take up to 1000–2000ms[15].

3. Once successfully established, the radio can now start to transmit data.

4. Now packets of data are transferred from the radio to the tower (called the **radio resource controller** or RRC). This is called user-plane, one-way latency[16]. It's the first wireless hop that each device has to go through. This can take up to 5ms on a 4G network.

---

[11] http://chimera.labs.oreilly.com/books/1230000000545/ch07.html
[12] http://en.wikipedia.org/wiki/Electromagnetic_interference
[13] http://en.wikipedia.org/wiki/Co-channel_interference
[14] http://en.wikipedia.org/wiki/Interference_(communication)
[15] https://www.igvita.com/2012/07/19/latency-the-new-web-performance-bottleneck/
[16] http://chimera.labs.oreilly.com/books/1230000000545/ch07.html#_initiating_a_request

5. Once arrived at the RRC, the packets of data will be sent to the core network (CN). The CN connects the tower to the worldwide Web to establish the request for the website. Part of the CN represents a public gateway that connects the mobile carrier to the public Internet.

As you can surmise, latency is an unfortunate factor when dealing with wireless communications. Consequently it is important to keep the number of HTTP requests as small as possible to avoid any further latency issues. It's better to send fewer HTTP requests with bigger responses than many HTTP requests with smaller responses.

The table below[17] shows how much latency typically comes with requesting HTTP assets over mobile networks for active mobile connections:

| Mobile Generation | Data Rate | Latency |
| --- | --- | --- |
| 2G | 100–400kbit/s | 300–1000ms |
| 3G | 0.5–5Mbit/s | 100–500ms |
| 4G | 1–50Mbit/s | < 100ms |

Latency variability can be very high on mobile networks and carriers. While 4G networks will improve latency[18], it will be a while before all mobile users have switched to 4G networks.

## CPU/GPU and Less Memory

CPU stands for **central processing unit,** the brain of all computers including mobile devices. Today's mobile devices offer processing power roughly equivalent to that of a desktop computer from five or more years ago.

GPU stands for **graphics processing unit**. Its main function is to offload graphics tasks that would otherwise be processed and calculated by the main CPU. The architecture of the GPU is designed solely around graphic processing—and, as a result, it can accomplish this task more efficiently than the CPU.

The more we load on the CPU/GPU—especially on smaller devices such as smartphones—the more they have to work, resulting in slower processing and poorer

---

[17] Source: *High Performance Browser Networking* by Ilya Grigorik

[18] https://www.igvita.com/slides/2013/breaking-1s-mobile-barrier.pdf

performance. Developers who've become accustomed to the huge memory available on desktop and laptop computers should remember that the memory capacity of mobile devices is drastically less. The less memory available, the more challenging performance becomes. As mentioned in Chapter 6, certain JavaScript operations come with a performance price, and any major manipulations of the DOM could cause memory problems for mobile devices.

## Slower JavaScript Execution

Everything feels slower on mobile devices. Their JavaScript engines are a lot slower than their desktop counterparts. DOM manipulations and other expensive operations keep the GPU and CPU busy. For example, Flickr encountered a major issue[19] on the mobile version of their site when they implemented their first version of a slideshow. The iOS browser would constantly crash when displaying more than 20 images. The cause for the crash? Flickr coded too many manipulations of the DOM, resulting in the CPU and GPU not being able to keep up with it anymore.

# Power Consumption and Data Plans

In addition to recognizing the performance constraints of mobile devices, it's important to consider the power and data consumption of mobile devices when developing a lean website.

## Battery Consumption

Mobile devices run off a battery, which drains faster the more work the device has to do. A lean website should aim to minimize the battery drain of mobile devices.

The following results came out of some excellent research[20] conducted by academics from Stanford University and Deutsche Telekom Research & Development in Los Altos. Their research evaluated the energy level of mobile devices based on browsing the Internet.

- **Images:** rendering images takes a significant fraction of the total rendering energy. Compressing images to JPEG has shown improvements on energy consumption.

---

[19] http://code.flickr.net/2011/07/20/lessons-learned-from-the-flickr-touch-lightbox/
[20] http://www2012.wwwconference.org/proceedings/proceedings/p41.pdf

- **JavaScript:** JavaScript is one of the most energy-consuming components in a web page. Remove as many unused frameworks or manipulations as possible.

- **CSS:** the rendering cost of CSS depends on the number of items styled. Concatenating CSS files also helps to reduce energy consumption.

This all sounds a bit familiar, doesn't it? I've already mentioned these things when we discussed optimizing websites in general. So by following these rules, we can ensure that our website will also be energy-efficient on mobile.

## Data Consumption

Data plans still remain expensive[21] in several countries, especially when traveling. The leaner a site's assets, the less data consumption being forced on users.

There's a sobering example of the effect a poorly optimized site can have on mobile data usage. Mobiforge[22] ran an experiment on cellular data charges. They took a SIM from a European cellular provider and used it on an Android phone while roaming in the US. Loading just one web page[23] with a size of around 10MB cost around €369, or approximately US$480[24].

# Device Management

Various organizations have created repositories of information about the currently available portable devices. The goal is to help you detect devices based on a variety of factors, such as their features, screen-size, or operating system. Most organizations offering such a **device description repository** (DDR) charge for access to their data, offering a free version with limited access. Commercial versions normally come with additional features, such as detection for multiple websites, local solutions, and unlimited detections per month.

Let's look at several of the DDR products on offer.

---

[21] http://www.wallcom.ca/pdfs/price-comp-report_2013update.pdf

[22] http://mobiforge.com/

[23] http://www.briefcakes.com/gallery.html

[24] http://mobiforge.com/research-analysis/performance-money-part-1-end-users-wallet

# WURFL

WURFL[25] stands for Wireless Universal Resource File. It's a big XML file listing details of all of the devices available. The repository used to be free and open-source, until it was commercialized in 2011.

Based on the HTTP user agent string, you can match and profile a device that accesses your site using WURFL. It not only lists all devices and specifications, but also provides grouping and categorization—making it easier for you to "bucket" certain devices by their capabilities.

Here is a sample snippet of the WURFL `device` node for an iPhone 4 entry:

```
<device id="apple_generic" user_agent="Mozilla/5.0 (iPhone; U; CPU
➡ iPhone OS 4_0 like Mac OS X; xx-xx) AppleWebKit/532.9 (KHTML,
➡ like Gecko) Version/4.0.5 Mobile/8A293 Safari/6531.22.7"
➡ fall_back="generic_xhtml">
    <group id="product_info">
      <capability name="mobile_browser" value="Safari"/>
      <capability name="device_os" value="iOS"/>
      <capability name="has_qwerty_keyboard" value="true"/>
      <capability name="pointing_method" value="touchscreen"/>
      <capability name="is_tablet" value="false"/>
      <capability name="model_name" value="iPhone"/>
      <capability name="device_os_version" value="4.0"/>
      <capability name="is_wireless_device" value="true"/>
    </group>
    <!-- ... -->
    <group id="display">
      <capability name="physical_screen_height" value="74"/>
      <capability name="resolution_width" value="320"/>
      <capability name="resolution_height" value="480"/>
    </group>
  <!-- ... -->
</device>
```

Based on the above criteria, you could target all iPhone users by validating the `model_name` to match the incoming user agent string of your users.

---

[25] http://en.wikipedia.org/wiki/WURFL

> ### WURFL Explorer
>
> Try out the WURFL explorer[26] to examine descriptions of many devices in the WURFL DDR.

The WURFL DDR file has grown tremendously over the last decade as more devices have been released. It's currently a 20MB XML file. Parsing this entire file every time you need to use it is not very efficient. I recommend filtering and shrinking the file according to your own needs.

If you decide to use WURFL, or its commercial ScientiaMobile[27] version, you can benefit from several server-side[28] and client-side[29] implementations. But if you don't want to use WURFL, for whatever reason, there are some other repositories available.

# Other DDRs

While WURFL was one of the first DDR products, there are other solutions that provide detailed information about your users' devices. There's no real stand-out winner here. Which you choose basically depends on your preference of programming language and your wallet.

## DeviceAtlas (Free and Commercial Versions)

DeviceAtlas[30] follows the same idea as WURFL: it gives you access to a huge database of mobile devices, spitting out any kind of information you need about these devices.

DeviceAtlas comes in several programming languages[31], such as Java, PHP, .NET, Python, Ruby, and JavaScript, and is also accessible directly via a REST API[32].

There's a trial version available that comes with an API key, or you can fall back to the free, cloud-based version of the product that comes with a device detection client only, offers a limit on detections per month, and is only available for one

---

[26] http://www.tera-wurfl.com/explore/?action=wurfl_id&id=apple_iphone_ver2
[27] http://www.scientiamobile.com/
[28] http://www.smashingmagazine.com/2014/07/01/server-side-device-detection-with-javascript/
[29] http://web.wurfl.io
[30] https://deviceatlas.com/
[31] https://deviceatlas.com/resources
[32] https://deviceatlas.com/resources/rest-api

website. The enterprise version (local version available) offers unrestricted access to carrier identification and a device properties list[33] that is otherwise restricted for the cloud version.

The DeviceAtlas Data Explorer[34] gives you a good overview of what kind of data and device properties you can receive from this service.

The following code snippet shows part of the output after passing in the user agent string for an iPhone 4 to inquire about its device properties:

```
$ php device.php
$ --------------------------------------------------------------
    All Properties:
    3gp.aac.lc (boolean) : 1
    displayPpi (integer) :165
    js.supportBasicJavaScript (boolean) :1
    js.geoLocation (boolean) :  1
    flashCapable (boolean) :
    js.json (boolean) : 1
    isTablet (boolean) :
    isMobilePhone (boolean) :   1
    browserVersion (string) :   5.0.2
    osVersion (string) :    4_2_1
    browserName (string) :  Safari
    devicePixelRatio (string) : 1
    js.webSqlDatabase (boolean) :   1
    stream.httpLiveStreaming (boolean) :    1
    marketingName (string) :    iPhone
    ...
```

## DeviceMap (Free)

DeviceMap[35] is an open-source project by Apache. It aims to create a data repository that includes information on mobile devices. Like WURFL, the data is also stored in XML, but it's split up into several different files, based on device characteristics, browser, and vendor data.

---

[33] https://deviceatlas.com/resources/available-properties
[34] https://deviceatlas.com/device-data/explorer
[35] http://incubator.apache.org/devicemap/

DeviceMap supports Java, C#, VB.Net, and JavaScript. A web demo[36] is available, giving you a quick peak into what kind of information you can gather from the DDR:

```xml
<!-- DeviceDataSource.xml Snippet -->
<device id="iPhone" parentId="genericApple">
    <property name="model" value="iPhone"/>
    <property name="displayWidth" value="320"/>
    <property name="displayHeight" value="480"/>
    <property name="device_os_version" value="1.0"/>
    <property name="mobile_browser_version" value="5"/>
    <property name="from" value="open_db_modified"/>
</device>
```

## Create Your Own DDR

If you don't want somebody else to provide you with device information, you can just create your own list, stored in your own preferred format, such as XML, JSON and so on.

For example, on one project I was a part of, we categorized devices into various "buckets"—"dumb", "smart" and "touch". Devices with simple WAP browsers were classed as "dumb", more advanced devices with HTML browsers were "smart", and devices with advanced browsers and touch gestures were "touch" . We used these buckets to differentiate mobile devices by identifying them based on their user agent string (see the next section). Depending on which of those buckets the user's device fell into, we not only served different designs, but also different image sizes.

If your mobile strategy and buckets are easy to manage, and don't require a lot of detailed drilling, you may well be satisfied with using CSS media queries, and perhaps a bit of JavaScript.

However, while this all sounds like a great plan—as it's simple to set up and inexpensive compared to buying access to a commercial DDR—you need to understand the challenges that come with this approach. A major issue is that you'll need to maintain the list of available devices constantly, adding another burden to your task list that can very easily be overlooked. A possible solution could be to create a cron job to fetch new devices and user agent strings from either one of the commercial or open-source DDRs to keep your device repository up to date.

---

[36] http://devicemap-vm.apache.org/browsermap/index.html

# Device Detection

In order to utilize the information gleaned from the device repositories, we'll need to determine exactly what devices are hitting our website. This can be done by using several device detection methods.

## Take a Quick Inventory

Before you start using device detection on your website, my advice is to do a quick inventory of your current users and their devices. You can use a tool like Google Analytics to get this data.

For example, using Analytics on my personal website (bbinto.me) reveals that, during October, I had 23 different devices accessing my site, with 72 different screen resolutions.

Let's be realistic: you can't target all devices, screen resolutions, browsers and connection speeds. Yet all of those factors still play an important role in how your user will experience the performance, and quality, of your site. Instead of optimizing for every entry that pops up in Analytics, a good start is to pick the top five to ten entries in the lists you've gathered and focus on these.

Now, let's move on to how you can detect your users' devices.

## The Identifier: HTTP Header

HTTP headers—which are sent when the browser requests content—are the basis for device detection. The most interesting and useful header is the **user-agent** string. Using the user agent string to detect devices is called **user agent sniffing**. You can use the default Firefox developer tools to show and modify the user agent string, as shown in Figure 10.1:

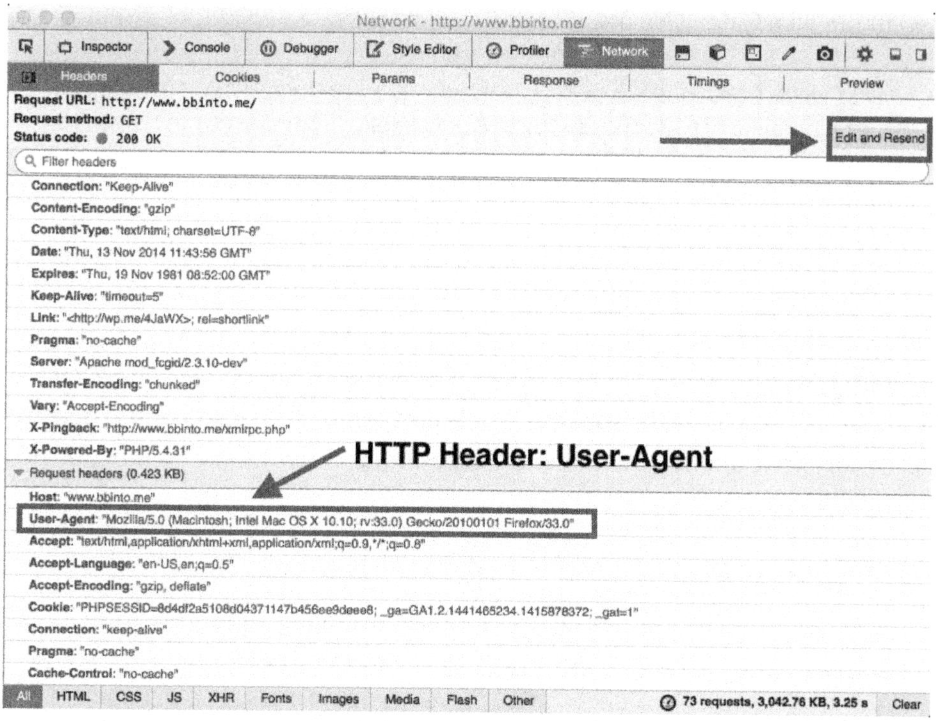

Figure 10.1. *Firefox developer tools' **Network** Panel view with HTTP headers*

With a user agent string, you're able to retrieve the version of the browser, the operating system, and the device.

Here is a sample of some commonly used devices and their user agent strings:

▢ Safari on iPhone 6:

```
Mozilla/5.0 (iPhone; CPU iPhone OS 6_1_3 like Mac OS X) AppleWeb
➡Kit/536.26 (KHTML, like Gecko) Version/6.0 Mobile/10B329 Safari
➡/8536.25
```

▢ Safari on iPad:

```
Mozilla/5.0 (iPad; CPU OS 7_0 like Mac OS X) AppleWebKit/537.51.1
➡ (KHTML, like Gecko) CriOS/30.0.1599.12 Mobile/11A465 Safari/
➡8536.25 (3B92C18B-D9DE-4CB7-A02A-22FD2AF17C8F)
```

- Chrome on a Galaxy Nexus:

```
Mozilla/5.0 (Linux; Android 4.1.1; Galaxy Nexus Build/JRO03O)
➥ AppleWebKit/535.19 (KHTML, like Gecko) Chrome/18.0.1025.166
➥ Mobile Safari/535.19
```

The basic idea behind device detection is to compare the incoming user agent string of your visitor's browser with a list you maintain. Using your preferred DDR—whether that's WURFL, DeviceAtlas, DeviceMap or your own filters—you can then start customizing the user experience based on the device's characteristics. The biggest advantage of device detection is that content becomes context-sensitive. We can serve different content to users depending on their device's functionality and capabilities.

There are various options for executing device detection:

- **Server-side**: the detection happens on the server, by deciding what to serve to the client before it lands in the browser.

- **CDN**: the detection is done on the CDN level, without having to go back to the origin to receive content.

- *Client-side*: the detection is executed once the browser receives the content. Unnecessary content might have been served by that time.

- *Client Hints*: this approach is not fully supported yet, but it is the most promising and efficient way of serving the right content, and functionality, to different devices. It's a hybrid of client- and server-side solutions.

## Server-side Options

There are several discussions in the web community over what approach to use when building performant (mobile) websites, or web apps. On one hand, there's the notion of first sending everything needed to the browser, and then letting the client decide what to display. The advantage of this approach is that, once everything has arrived at the client's end, browsing the site is faster, as all the necessary assets have already been sent down the wire. But on the other hand, you could also let the server decide what content to display *before* even sending it to the client—serving only the absolutely necessary assets on first load. This improves the time to first byte and initial load time, with more assets subsequently being fetched as needed. Server-side programming languages like PHP, Perl, ASP.NET, Java, Python—or even Edge Side Includes, sitting on the CDN—can be used to detect your users' devices.

My advice is that, if you can do the device detection on the server, choose this over client-side detection. Anything you tell your browser to do once the page has arrived only costs power, time, and data.

Here are some useful tools for server-side device detection:

- Detect Mobile Browsers[37] is a great resource for mobile detection, offering many client-side and server-side solutions.

- 51 Degrees[38] provides a device management system, as well as device detection, in most common server-side programming languages.

- Apache Mobile Filter[39] is an Apache-based filter for detecting mobile devices.

## CDN Options

Edge Side Includes[40] (ESI) is an XML-based markup language. ESI support is offered by CDN vendors like Akamai, F5 and Varnish. If you use any of these vendors, you have ESI at your disposal. ESI can be used for caching purposes, which will ultimately help you with mobile performance.

If you're familiar with Server Side Includes[41] (SSI) and XML/XSLT, you'll have no problem understanding ESI. It supports access to variables based on HTTP request attributes. For example, you can easily check for any field in the HTTP_HEADER, and hence also for the HTTP_USER_AGENT attribute.

ESI can also include snippets of additional content via an include command. To make this even more powerful, ESI supports conditional processing, which means logic can be applied to execute specific content via an include, based on specific conditions like user agent strings. For example, you could include a map just for GPS capable devices, or only show a big video on desktop devices. All of this is

---

[37] http://detectmobilebrowsers.com/
[38] http://51degrees.com/Support/Documentation
[39] http://fiftyone.apachemobilefilter.org/
[40] http://www.w3.org/TR/esi-lang
[41] http://en.wikipedia.org/wiki/Server_Side_Includes

done by the edge server—the server that is closest to the user. Users will never get content they're not supposed to receive, and no data is sent down the wire that isn't required. Additionally, when processing ESI, there's no need to go back to the origin for processing, and thus the load at the origin is cut down.

You can create a device list by assigning a regular expression to an ESI variable, and use this to detect user agent strings, like this:

```
<esi:comment text="Regular expression to match tablets' user
➥ agents"/>
<esi:assign name="tablet" value="'(iPad|Nexus 10|PlayBook|Xoom|hp-
➥tablet|Dell Streak)'"/>
```

You could use WURFL, or any other device catalog, to populate this variable automatically, based on the latest devices and your defined criteria.

## Client-side Options

Client-side device detection is executed on the client, thus working with already-delivered content. If you've decided to use a client-side approach, you can easily detect the user agent string by requesting the value of `navigator.userAgent` in JavaScript.

Detect Mobile Browsers offers client-side options. Device.js[42] is another, small (3KB) and solid JavaScript solution for detecting devices, and targeting the user experience based on that.

## Client Hints

Most solutions discussed so far come with a price: you either have to use your web server (potentially relying on commercial DDRs), leverage your CDN for device detection features, or (if you can't do either of these), use client-side options to do the heavy lifting.

Client Hints[43] will land some time in the near future, offering a hybrid client/server-side solution. But how will it work? The user agent information stored in the HTTP header is used by Client Hints to make decisions about resources to be loaded for

---

[42] https://github.com/matthewhudson/device.js/
[43] https://github.com/igrigorik/http-client-hints

this specific client. The user agent gives the server hints on its capabilities, and hence won't be asked to load resources that it doesn't require—resulting in reduced overhead, as the logic is executed on the server.

The current implementation status for Client Hints notes that IE is considering[44] the implementation, while Mozilla has filed a bug report[45] on it. The entire draft[46] can be found on the IETF website.

## Disadvantages of User Agent Sniffing

All of the approaches mentioned above rely on the user agent; and although the user agent is today's go-to solution for detecting a visitor's device, pure user agent sniffing suffers from several disadvantages:

- The user agent string doesn't include any information about—for example—the device's screen width or height, and therefore can't reliably identify all static variables.

- In order to adapt and optimize content for different devices, the user agent detection requires a device database that can be costly to maintain.

- User agent detection is not cache friendly, and therefore has to be executed every time the user visits your page.

- User agent strings are not structured data and can be modified. (Some devices even lie about their true identity!)

# Device Testing

Nowadays, it's not enough to simply test your website on a range of desktop browsers, such as Chrome, Safari, Firefox, Opera or Internet Explorer. The multi-device macrocosm has added more challenges for us—different devices with different capabilities, different screen sizes, and many different connection speeds. We now have to plan for these challenges when building websites. If you work in a bigger company, you might be lucky enough to have access to a device lab with many different

---

[44] https://status.modern.ie/httpclienthints?term=client%20hints
[45] https://bugzilla.mozilla.org/show_bug.cgi?id=935216
[46] https://tools.ietf.org/html/draft-grigorik-http-client-hints-02

devices. If not, I'll share some tips on how to get your website tested on a range of devices.

It's virtually impossible to test every single device or screen size out there. You can use the device inventory you've created, as described earlier, to help you set a baseline for what you're going to support. If you don't currently use analytics or tracking, now is the time to do it. The data it provides is extremely helpful in optimizing your performance.

Once you've established the device list you want to support, you can start testing.

# Simulators

There are various simulators you can use to simulate your web pages on different devices. Here's a selection:

- User Agent Switcher[47] is a browser extension that can simulate different user agent strings, thus helping to debug various issues on the spot. Switching the user agent to a mobile device will help you simulate how your website looks on a mobile browser. There are other browser extensions for mimicking a different user agent. And recent versions of Chrome come with a user agent switcher built in.

- BrowserStack[48] is a commercial, online tool that's really handy if you can't afford to build a physical device lab. You can test your website on many different browsers, and debug your HTML, CSS and JavaScript with the handy developer tools included.

- WebPagetest[49] is the silver bullet for everything performance related. Depending on the test location you choose, you can select one of several device and browser options. You can obviously only test one page of your site at a time, but this might sometimes be enough. The synthetic WPT result will help you understand how your site is performing on mobile. However, you probably wouldn't use it for debugging, as it's static and won't allow user interaction.

---

[47] http://chrispederick.com/work/user-agent-switcher/
[48] http://www.browserstack.com/
[49] http://webpagetest.org

To simulate different connection speeds, you can use Chrome's developer tools, Slowy[50] or Wireshark[51].

## Real Device Testing

If you can build a device lab of real devices, like Etsy has[52], the following tools can help you facilitate testing on those devices:

- Adobe Edge Inspect[53] helps you live-test your website on multiple browsers by pairing your testing devices with your computer.

- Shim[54], running as a Node.js application, is similar to Adobe Edge Inspect, being able to load a page simultaneously on several devices that are connected to the same WiFi network.

### Simulator vs. Real Device Testing

It's always better to test on real devices than on simulators, especially if you have made a conscious decision to support specific browsers and device OSs. Simulators can't provide a proper simulation of battery consumption, for example, or of connection speed, or performance, and they can't replicate a touch screen experience with a mouse. So while they can be handy for simple testing purposes, don't put too much faith in them. Of course, you have to balance this consideration with the cost and logistics of testing a range of different devices.

## Cool Down

- Mobile usage is on the rise, and browsing via mobile devices will soon surpass desktop browsing.

- Particular challenges for mobile are speed, battery life and power consumption. When developing mobile websites, assume the worst connection for your user.

---

[50] http://slowyapp.com/
[51] https://www.wireshark.org/
[52] https://codeascraft.com/2013/08/09/mobile-device-lab/
[53] https://creative.adobe.com/products/inspect
[54] https://github.com/dmolsen/shim

- Device description repositories are regularly updated lists of the many devices on the market, and can be used to identify the devices being used to connect with your site.

- You can detect devices based on the HTTP user agent string header, either via server-side or client-side solutions.

- There are some helpful tools for testing (or simulating) your website on mobile devices.

# Mobile Optimization Techniques

## Warm Up

In the last chapter, we discussed some of the performance challenges posed by the mobile web. Let's take a look at how to address those challenges, by running through some performance boosters that can help make a mobile website lean and fast. At the end of the chapter, I'll present you with some ideas on how to create your own mobile strategy.

## Mobile Performance Boosters

Let's start by examining options for improving mobile web browsing.

### Offline Storage

HTML5 introduced offline storage[1], which makes it possible for browsers to store a copy of a web page, thus allowing users to browse the page while offline. Offline storage can help save unnecessary HTTP requests by removing the need to re-fetch

---

[1] http://www.html5rocks.com/en/features/storage

assets from the server. Importantly, in the context of this book, offline storage also helps to improve *perceived* performance.

While offline storage can be somewhat buggy[2], and sometimes tricky to implement and manage, there are web applications—such as the Financial Times Web App[3] or Google's web-based offline email[4] version—that have shown how to use it successfully for performance enhancements. Imagine yourself on a train, wanting to finish reading a news article before going underground. If the website supports offline storage, you can continue reading without interruption.

Offline browsing can be realized by using either the "application cache" (often abbreviated to "appcache") or "local storage", both of which help in avoiding HTTP requests, because they cache and save files locally.

**Appcache**[5] allows you to specify which files the browser should cache and make available to offline users. It's based on a **manifest file** that tells the browser what to load from a local cache versus what files to request freshly. However, you need to think about what files should be saved locally. Since appcache still unreliable in certain browsers, it's best to follow the advice from the FT Labs[6] team and keep the manifest file as small as possible, and only include fairly small files such as fonts, favicons, and a few images.

**Local storage**[7] is also referred to as "client-side storage" or "web storage". It's based on key–value pairs like any JavaScript object. You can store blocks of JavaScript or CSS in local storage, and on subsequent page views you can retrieve these blocks and insert them into the page, resulting in a smaller HTML document download size, and a faster Start Render time.

The Guardian[8] website shows an example of how to use local storage to boost performance. It includes some JavaScript that's executed if the visitor's browser supports local storage. The CSS file is asynchronously loaded via Ajax. On the first run, the

---

[2] http://alistapart.com/article/application-cache-is-a-douchebag

[3] http://apps.ft.com/ftwebapp/

[4] http://googlecode.blogspot.com/2009/04/gmail-for-mobile-html5-series-using.html

[5] https://developer.mozilla.org/en-US/docs/Web/HTML/Using_the_application_cache

[6] http://www.smashingmagazine.com/2013/05/23/building-the-new-financial-times-web-app-a-case-study/

[7] http://diveintohtml5.info/storage.html

[8] http://www.theguardian.com/

CSS is included inline, but also stored in the browser's local storage. Next time the user visits the page, or any subsequent pages on the Guardian website, the server won't load the inline CSS again, but instead will use the local storage version, allowing the page to be served faster to the user. By using this method, the Guardian was able to drop its Start Render time from 1.113s to 0.759s[9].

### Storage Limitations

If you're planning to store large amounts of data, be aware that most mobile browsers can't store more than approximately 5MB in local storage.

Other local storage techniques you could use include Web SQL Database[10] (deprecated), IndexedDB[11], and the File System API[12]. You should consider using a structured database rather than local storage if you want to store a lot of content, because local storage can become slow when performing multiple operations. Also, local storage is executed synchronously, whereas the database options are asynchronous, allowing you to fetch data in parallel, and thus avoid blocking the execution of your mobile application.

# Other Mobile-specific Optimization Tips

All of the performance boosters we discussed in Chapter 5, Chapter 6 and Chapter 7 are helpful for mobile websites. But as we discussed in Chapter 10, the higher latency on mobile networks, and less powerful CPUs/GPUs of mobile devices (which leads to slower JavaScript performance), both create special challenges for web performance on mobile devices. Let's go through some tips on how to optimize your website with a specific focus on mobile constraints.

## Fighting Mobile Latency

Don't allow the mobile device's radio to move in and out of idle mode too often, in order to avoid unnecessary round trips. When in an idle state, the device isn't able to send or receive any data. To send and receive data, the radio must synchronize with a nearby radio tower, which requires several round trips between the mobile

---

[9] https://speakerd.s3.amazonaws.com/presentations/ca037050b8d40131e4494251e58a135f/Breaking_news_at_1000ms_-_4-3_-_pdf.pdf
[10] http://www.w3.org/TR/webdatabase/
[11] http://www.w3.org/TR/IndexedDB/
[12] http://www.w3.org/TR/file-system-api/

device and the tower. As a result, switching between the idle and non-idle states not only reduces battery life, but also introduces more latency, which in turn affects performance.

Therefore, try to execute all your requests as quickly as possible, in a single batch, and then allow the radio to return to idle. Try to use the radio while it's already fired up—for example, by using pre-fetching techniques we've discussed previously.

In addition, fight latency on mobile by reducing HTTP requests as much as possible, and compress and cache assets to circumvent any further requests or round trips.

 **Domain Sharding**

The idea behind **domain sharding**[13] is to split assets across multiple domains or subdomian in order to serve them faster to the user. The browser can open up to six concurrent connections, allowing your assets to be spread across six different domains, which can be downloaded in parallel. Don't be fooled by this approach, however. In particular with regard to mobile websites, with different domains, there aer additional DNS lookups and additional TCP connections that have to be opened. If you use more than two domains[14], performance suffers, especially when your mobile user doesn't have enough bandwidth to handle this shower of assets from the server.

## Optimizing Repaints and Reflows

JavaScript execution can be slower on mobile devices, so avoid repaint and reflow operations as much as possible, and avoid too many DOM manipulations. Chapter 5 has more details on how to enhance repaints and reflows.

## Jank-free Scrolling and Animations

Most mobile devices nowadays use touch gestures, where fingers do the scrolling. Finger gestures make it easy to scroll fast through pages. As discussed in Chapter 5, animations should ideally run at 60 frames per second for a smooth result. However, due to the CPU/GPU constraints on mobile, processing animations can take several hundred milliseconds. During this time, an animation may become hopelessly "janky", especially when scrolling fast.

---

[13] http://www.stevesouders.com/blog/2009/05/12/sharding-dominant-domains/
[14] http://www.stevesouders.com/blog/2013/09/05/domain-sharding-revisited/

To produce smooth animations on mobile devices, I recommended using `request-AnimationFrame()` (discussed in Chapter 6). You'll save CPU cycles this way, the animations being better synced with your GPU. This will also help preserve your user's battery life.

# Content Presentation

The following section outlines three different approaches to serving content to mobile users: the dedicated mobile ("mdot") site; the single-URL, responsive site; and the RESS site, a kind of hybrid.

Firstly, I'll explain what they are and how to set them up. Then I'll present a comparison of the approaches, to help you decide which will achieve the best performance results for your site.

## Dedicated Mobile Website, or mdot

An **mdot** website is a separate version of a site geared specifically for mobile devices. Its name refers to the typical URL scheme used on such websites, such as m.example.com.

The main advantage of the mdot approach is **content adaptation**. Before sending the user the site content, the server detects the kind of device making the request, and automatically redirects from the desktop to the mdot site. No heavy desktop-specific content (such as big images) will be sent to the user. The content is organized and presented specifically for mobile devices.

However, by including a redirect, you add an additional DNS lookup to process, which could increase the overall page load time. Also, being a separate website, the effort to maintain, design, and keep both versions in sync needs to be considered and planned for.

If you decide to use an mdot site, make sure you properly add code in the page's head to help search engines like Google understand what version of the site to send to your visitors. For the desktop version, put this in the head:

```
<link rel="alternate" media="only screen and (max-width: 640px)"
    href="http://m.example.com/hello">
```

For the corresponding mobile site, put this in the `head`:

```
<link rel="canonical" href="http://www.example.com/hello">
```

# Redirects

Before redirecting users to the mobile version of your site, you'll need to detect their device properly. Redirects are part of the mdot website process, and users only need to know the main (non-mdot) URL of your site. Once typed into the browser, the server will direct users to the appropriate site depending on their device. It's important that you think about URL naming conventions. By having a clean, structured URL hierarchy, it will be easier for you to map between the corresponding websites—for example, example.com/section1 could either correspond to m.example.com/section1 or example.com/m/section1.

### Skipping the Redirect

Avoid making the user go through the redirect over and over again when accessing the site via mobile. You can mitigate the redirect delay by encouraging users to bookmark the mobile version, either as a regular bookmark, or by adding it to their home screen.

Before discussing redirect techniques, let's check out some real-world examples of websites that use an mdot approach, and the delays caused due to the redirects. I took screenshots of the waterfall for LinkedIn (Figure 11.1) and Facebook (Figure 11.1) on mobile devices via WPT, and tested the desktop URLs with a WPT mobile device:

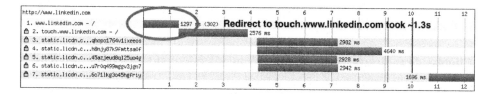

Figure 11.1. LinkedIn[15] on mobile, redirect from linkedin.com to touch.www.linkedin.com, wasting 1.3s just for the redirect

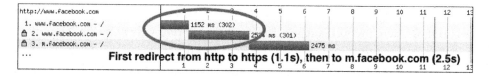

Figure 11.2. Facebook[16] on mobile, redirect from facebook.com to m.facebook.com, taking around 3.6s just for two redirects

For the Facebook example, there are two redirect hoops the user has to jump through before landing on the mdot site:

1. The first redirect of 1.1s is to redirect from http:// to https://

2. Then it takes around 2.5 seconds to redirect to m.facebook.com

3. Only then, after approximately 3.6 seconds, does the user get to the intended destination.

## Redirect Methods

There are three primary methods for directing users to the appropriate location:

▪ **Server-side redirects:** this can be done by simple server rewrite rules. You can tell Apache, Nginx, IIS or other web servers how to redirect users based on their user agent. In addition, server-side languages such as PHP can also be utilized to handle the redirects based on the user agent.

▪ **ESI redirects:** running off the CDN network, ESI redirects are very useful and can be set up based on user agent strings. All of this is done at the edge; users will never get content they are not supposed to receive. Additionally, when

---

[15] http://www.webpagetest.org/result/141102_GK_F1K/

[16] http://www.webpagetest.org/result/141102_RS_F2Y/

processing ESI, there is no need to go back to the origin for processing, and thus the load at the origin is cut down.

■ **Client-side redirects:** the redirect is done via client-side scripting, such as JavaScript. The entire page is sent to the user before any validation, selection or detection has been executed.

So, which of these methods should you choose?

Normally, server-side redirects are faster than client-side redirects, so if it's choice between these two, I would suggest focusing on a server-side solution. However, if you use a CDN and ESI is supported, I'd consider this to be the preferred option, because the ESI redirect offers an additional advantage over regular server-side redirects: it occurs at the edge, and is faster than putting the redirect logic at the origin.

Client-side redirects are the least-preferred solution in my opinion, because anything that the client has to figure out, such as JavaScript execution, affects the performance, battery power and CPU consumption of the device.

No matter what redirect method you choose, remember not to limit users to only viewing the mobile version of the site. Always give them the option to override the redirect policy and view the full site, because people don't like to be forced into things!

## Responsive Websites

Besides offering a dedicated mdot site, there's another, quite different approach to optimizing your site for mobile devices. Google's mobile best practices[17] suggest that web developers should create responsive websites. **Responsive web design** (RWD), coined by Ethan Marcotte in 2010, centers on the idea of serving the one same HTML page to all devices. There's only one version of the site, but it's *styled* differently for different devices. RWD relies on CSS3 media queries, fluid grids, and flexible images. A media query serves up specially targeted styles when the browser window is below (or above) a certain defined width. The transition points specified by the media queries are known as **breakpoints**.

---

[17] https://developers.google.com/webmasters/smartphone-sites/

In order for a website to transition as described, the layout must be flexible. Fluid grids are designed by using variable measurements, such as percentages, instead of pixels, so the elements inside the grid container can adjust according to the parent container's size. Images are also sized in relative units to keep them flexible and always contained within their parent element.

Here are some examples of how to use media queries. You can either use the `media` attribute within a `link` element, or `@media` in the style sheet itself.

- External style sheets loaded via a media query: in the example below, `mobile.css` will be used on any device with a width below 321px; `portrait.css` will be used instead on any device in portrait mode; and `print.css` will be used when the page is being printed:

```
<link rel="stylesheet" media="(max-width: 320px)" href=
➥"mobile.css">
<link rel="stylesheet" media="(orientation: portrait)" href=
➥"portrait.css">
<link rel="stylesheet" media="print" href="print.css">
```

### Possible Performance Cost

This technique comes with a performance cost. Most browsers will download all[18] CSS files even if the media query returns false, as shown in Figure 11.3:

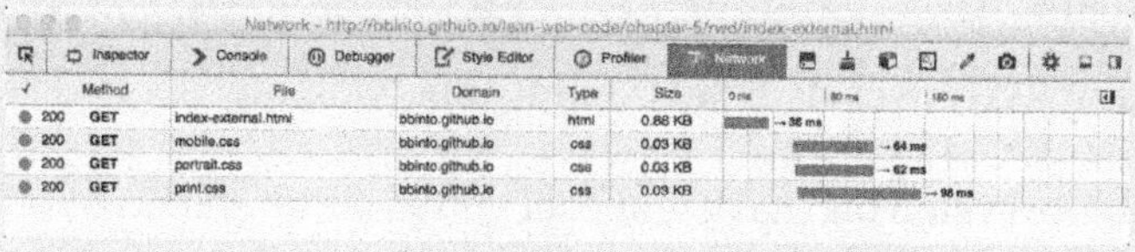

Figure 11.3. All three CSS files are being downloaded by the browser, no matter what media the user actually matches with

Instead of wasting these additional HTTP requests, put the styles into one CSS file, as seen below. If you still want to have structure and separation in your style sheets, keep separate files during development, but then concatenate into one at deployment to save additional HTTP requests.

---

[18] http://scottjehl.github.io/CSS-Download-Tests/

■ Here's as example of the same `@media` directives as above, this time included within the style sheet itself:

```
@media (max-device-width: 320px) {
  /* mobile styles */
}
@media (orientation: portrait) {
    /* portrait styles */
}
@media print {
    /* print styles */
}
```

Research by Guy Podjarny[19] shows that most responsive websites don't yet focus on web performance: 72% of the sites using responsive design don't optimize for mobile. While being viewed on small-screen devices, those pages have the same page weight as the ones being viewed on a large-screen device. Try to avoid sacrificing performance over convenience, because performance remains key for mobile websites.

In general, it might seem easier to optimize a mobile website for performance than a RWD website. Let's compare the advantages and disadvantages of responsive web design.

## RWD Advantages

Advantages of RWD over dedicated mdot sites include:

■ **Cross-platform sharing**: have you ever gotten a link shared by a friend, and when you open it on your laptop, it opens up the mobile version? With RWD, you only share one URL, and don't have to worry what version will be shown to the user.

■ **Search engine optimization (SEO)**: Google indicates[20] that responsive web design is its "recommended design pattern." A responsive website only has one URL with (normally) the same content for all devices. Thus, Google will have an easier job crawling and indexing your content.

---

[19] http://www.guypo.com/real-world-rwd-performance-take-2/

[20] https://developers.google.com/webmasters/mobile-sites/mobile-seo/overview/select-config

■ **Fewer codebases to maintain**: consolidated work into one web property comes with some maintenance advantages, one codebase serving all device properties.

## RWD Disadvantages

Responsive websites can be less efficient that mdot sites, as they sometimes serve content to mobile devices that's not needed:

**Download and `display: none`**    For smaller devices, not all the content should be shown. Consequently, content needs to be removed or, as is the case of most RWD sites, just not displayed. However, not displaying something doesn't mean it's not served to the client. As we learned in Chapter 5, anything on the critical rendering path with `display: none` will still be loaded into the rendering tree. You are basically only hiding assets visually while still asking the browser to download them—which isn't cool!

**Duplication of DOM Elements**    When developing a RWD site, a lot of logic is put into the code to handle and shuffle around boxes and containers, which results in the DOM inevitably getting bigger and more complex. The more code, the bigger the download, and the more work for the browser to construct the page on screen.

**Download and Resize**    Remember how we discussed that we should serve the appropriate image size to users? Well, this becomes a challenge for RWD. You want to show a nice image for a small screen, but you don't want to give up the quality and size for it to be shown on a bigger screen. What do you do? Sacrifice size for beauty and load the bigger image, but scale it down for the small screen? Considering that images are one of the big performance challenges, we shouldn't be doing this at all.

So for now, here are my two cents: based on statistics, I'm not convinced I would use RWD over a dedicated mdot site if speed and user experience are the things I care about the most. However, if you can't pay for a dedicated mobile site, I can recommend RWD, but only by following the best practices.

### Responsive Images to the Rescue?

There has been a movement in the performance community to address the problem of RWD sites being heavier than dedicated mobile sites. As we've discussed earlier, images are the main culprit for heavy websites. Responsive images aim to serve optimized images to RWD websites, removing unnecessary, bloated images for smaller devices.

The idea behind a responsive image is that the browser will display the image intelligently, choosing from a number of versions of the image based on the capabilities of the device. Conceptually, the image responds to the current device it's displayed in, and changes its dimensions and file size accordingly.

The Responsive Images Community Group[21] lists several approaches to serving images appropriately to different devices. Guy Podjarny's *Responsive & Fast: Implementing High-Performance Responsive Design*[22] also outlines best practices on using responsive images.

The good news is that this is a great step towards serving the right image size to the right device, and downloading only a smaller image if that's all that's required. The bad news is, not all browsers support responsive images yet.

Both mdot and RWD have their performance advantages and disadvantages. The next section describes a hybrid approach that combines the best of both methods.

# RESS

RESS stands for **Responsive Web Design with Server Side Components**[23], and refers to the use of responsive design in combination with server-side components. It solves many of the issues with RWD, utilizing advantages of the mdot approach. The server-side components enable the offloading of unwanted content before serving it to the client, while media queries are still used to accomplish responsive layouts. There are two RESS approaches you can take, which are detailed below.

---

[21] http://responsiveimages.org/
[22] http://www.akamai.com/dl/akamai/responsive-and-fast-implementing-high-performance-responsive-design.pdf
[23] http://www.lukew.com/ff/entry.asp?1392

## Original RESS

RESS is my favorite approach for serving content to different devices. It combines the best of both worlds, as you can present one single URL for all devices, but create a situational experience like this:

■ Server-side components take care of any heavy lifting, or complicated calculations such as JavaScript libraries, page templates, and other functionalities.

■ Client-side components take care of anything more layout-specific, such as changing and moving boxes—mostly things that can easily be handled by media queries.

For example, imagine you have a website presenting news with text and images: the mobile and desktop versions should deliver the same content. Let's assume the desktop version includes a bigger header and footer, whereas the mobile version's header and footer are simpler and smaller, so basically just differently designed but with the same functionality. The images for desktop should be higher resolution than the mobile versions. A possible RESS approach to this scenario would be as follows:

**Server-side components**    Detect the device on the server, and deliver a different image based on the device. Let's assume we have a small version of an image stored as **s_photo1.jpg**, and the original size **photo1.jpg**.

The `<?=$device_prefix?>` is determined on the server, based on the device, and will be dynamically included once the page loads on the user's end. The following code is provided in PHP and shows what prefix should be served for an iPhone:

```php
<?php
    $ua=$_SERVER['HTTP_USER_AGENT'];
    $device_prefix = '';
    if(preg_match('/iphone/i',$ua)) {
```

```
        $device_prefix = 's_';
    }
?>
```

And this is how you would write the corresponding HTML code:

```
<img src="<?=$device_prefix?>photo1.jpg"
➥ alt="Example photo"/>
```

**Client-side components**

The client-side components can take care of the styling of the header and footer via media queries. These queries can be stored in a CSS file as follows (simplified for the sake of this example):

```
header {
    height:100px;
}

footer {
    height:60px;
}

@media (max-device-width : 560px) {
    header {
        height:50px;
    }
    footer {
        height:20px;
    }

}
```

# RESS with ESI

As mentioned earlier, ESI can be a powerful tool for dealing with device detection and direction, so why not combine RESS with ESI?

With ESI, it's also possible to serve one single URL for your desktop and mobile site. Based on the device the user is using to connect with your site, you can create a content and markup switch for the entire page:

```
<!--esi
<esi:choose>
<esi:when test="$(HTTP_USER_AGENT) matches_i $(mobile_ua)">
        <!-- Mobile head and body -->
    </esi:when>
      <esi:otherwise>
         <!-- Desktop head and body -->
    </esi:otherwise>
</esi:choose>
-->
```

The code snippet above demonstrates how easy it is to serve completely different markup and content to a mobile device.

# Comparison of Mobile Site Approaches

Each approach to optimizing content for mobile devices has advantages and disadvantages, and several factors need to be considered when deciding which to use. What is my budget? How many resources do I have to support the website moving forward? How important is it to serve my site's content differently on different devices and in different contexts?

Let's list each technique and describe its pros and cons:

| | Pros | Cons | Watch out |
|---|---|---|---|
| mdot | Focus on performance, content adaptation, delivering only what is needed. | Multiple URLs (not easy to share), device detection repository needed, potentially complicated redirect logic, content forking, redirect with | Constant updating of device filters. |

| | Pros | Cons | Watch out |
|---|---|---|---|
| | | additional loading time. | |
| RWD | One URL for all content, no redirects, easy to share, suggested by Google, better for SEO, no device repository required. | Careful planning involved, content served that is not required, potentially hurting performance. | Bloated websites with duplicated DOM elements and so on. |
| RESS (with ESI) | If required, one URL for all content, no redirects, easy to share. | Device detection or feature detection required. RESS with ESI: no need to go back to the origin for processing, hence load at the origin is cut down. | Constant updating of device filters. |

My advice is to use RESS with ESI where access to a CDN with ESI support is available. This approach provides the most flexibility, and is best able to determine what to serve to a specific platform or device.

# Cool Down

- Various techniques such as offline storage are useful for improving perceived performance and reducing latency on mobile devices.

- The user agent HTTP header can be used to manage and detect devices.

- Three main options—mdot, RWD and RESS—exist for serving content efficiently to mobile devices. As always with performance, your choice depends on your current needs and resources.

- If you choose RWD, don't just make the website responsive. Also pay attention to performance.

- Learn how to use media queries properly. Try to avoid practices like setting unwanted content to `display:none`, as the hidden content will still be downloaded onto the device.

- Bypass extensive client-side processing (JavaScript, and non-optimized, third-party scripts), and try to move the logic from the front-end to the back-end.

- Strive to create the best user experience based on the user's platform and device. Know device specific features, and pitfalls, and take advantage of that knowledge.

Chapter **12**

# Performance Cheat Sheet

## Warm Up

In this final chapter, I've compiled a list of the most important tips and tricks covered throughout this book. It's designed to be a kind of performance cheat sheet, or, if you prefer, a set of exercises to guide you in practicing web performance. The more frequently you apply the tips below, the better you'll get at mastering performance issues and creating fast, lean websites.

## Shape a Performance Culture

This book has highlighted the importance of building a strong performance culture[1]. Make sure to bring everybody on board within your team and company. If you don't create the right culture, there'll be a constant performance battle with cross-functional teams such as product, marketing or design. You need to foster, educate and stand up for the idea that performance results in success, revenue, customer happiness and satisfaction. So foster web performance as part of your company's culture.

---

[1] http://www.stevesouders.com/blog/2013/05/17/creating-a-performance-culture/

## Team Culture Checklist

- Make *everybody* aware that performance is *everybody's* business, from product manager to content strategist, from designer to developer.

- Encourage, and feel encouraged, to say "No". Evaluate if a new script, or a big, heavy image, will really improve the customer experience and result in more revenue, and balance this against the performance hit the page might take because of this specific choice.

- Once performance gains have been made and identified, communicate, celebrate, and share this success frequently with the teams.

# Performance Is about Perception *and* Respect

Page size or page load time are not the only indicators of performance. Perceived performance is essential for a happy user. People won't notice when your site is fast, but they'll notice when it loads slowly. We should show our users respect by serving the content they requested as fast as possible. Don't make them wait!

## End User Checklist

- Ask the question "How long does it take for the user to interact with my page?" or "How many steps does it take the user to achieve this task?" Optimize based on these answers.

- Show respect to your visitors by avoiding any unnecessary delays in loading your page.

- Treat speed as a feature[2].

- Optimize *from* the user's perspective. Focus on the user's circumstances, and not your *ideal* setup. Record RUM data to discover the actual latency and connection speed of your users. Review Chapter 3 for details on synthetic and real user monitoring.

---

[2] https://www.igvita.com/slides/2013/io-pagespeed.pdf

▓ Your site is never fast enough: there's *always* room for improvement.

# Wireframing for Performance

Ensure that everybody in your team—including the designers and UX experts—understands how performance should be integrated, early on, into the design process. Chapter 2 covered some ideas on how to do that. Let's briefly summarize some of the most important tips.

## Planning Checklist

▓ Define and agree upon what's most important about your site, using the performance point system introduced in Chapter 2.

▓ Define measurable performance modules for each wireframe to illustrate performance impact.

▓ Agree on the above the fold content and prioritize visible content.

▓ Make an effort to explain performance implications to the entire team.

▓ Create a quick prototype to illustrate the performance impact of a proposed wireframe.

# Measure First, Then Optimize (and Repeat)

Talk numbers, show graphs and pie charts! Quantifying performance bottlenecks can have a huge impact on the website's decision makers. Use the tools and techniques introduced in Chapter 3 and Chapter 4, and practice the following guidelines.

## Measuring Checklist

▓ Choose your tools. Build your personal performance measurement arsenal by making use of powerful, open-source tools such as WebPagetest, PageSpeed Insights, RUM tools such as Boomerang, and the waterfall view of your browser. For tracking trends, check out HTTP Archive.

▓ Clean up your waterfall. Keep the overall waterfall as steep, thin and small as possible. Revisit Chapter 4 for more details.

- Set a performance budget to establish a goal to work towards, such as setting a baseline by comparing your performance results with those of your competitors.

- Before choosing third-party content (such as scripts), use the Resource Timing API introduced in Chapter 3 to measure their performance impact.

- Aim for a *low* Speed Index and a *high* PageSpeed value.

- Consider setting up a free private HTTP Archive, and WPT instance, for more control over a defined list of web pages and measurement cycles. Chapter 4 covered steps on how to get started.

# Determine Your Critical Rendering Path

Get to know and understand the critical rendering path of your page. Condense the code and resources required to render the initial view of a web page[3] as much as possible. Review the detailed example in Chapter 5 to help you apply some techniques and tools to optimize your critical rendering path.

## Critical Rendering Checklist

- HTML, the page itself, is always a critical resource. Keep it as clean as possible.

- Clean up your DOM by removing unused elements. They just delay the rendering process.

- Order matters: load critical assets as early as possible, and remove any render-blocking elements from the critical path.

- Don't put third-party features—such as scripts or web fonts—in your critical path.

- Minimize repaint and reflows, and avoid changing the appearance of an element without changing its layout, or changing the page layout. Revisit Chapter 6 for the list of CSS elements to avoid.

---

[3] https://developers.google.com/speed/docs/insights/mobile?csw=1#MinimizeDNSLookups

▪ Aim for 60fps or persistent frames of 30fps and higher for smooth scrolling. For animations, use `requestAnimationFrame()` instead of `setInterval()` or `set-Timeout()`, as explained in Chapter 6.

▪ Follow the 14KB rule to serve the most important content first.

▪ Prioritize visible content: focus on the above the fold content first, and load other assets afterwards.

▪ CSS is critical. Remove render-blocking CSS by using the media attribute (remembering, however, that the file will still be downloaded).

▪ The most important styles, especially above the fold styles, should go inline, as described in Chapter 5.

▪ Unblock the parser by using attributes such as `defer` or `async` for JavaScript tags.

▪ Put scripts at the bottom of the page to avoid render blocking.

▪ Make scripts non-blocking: wait until the `window.onload` event has fired to load less critical JavaScript files, and load them asynchronously, especially third-party scripts.

▪ Limit the total number of `script` tags to allow faster rendering. Review Chapter 6 for more JavaScript optimization tips.

# Reduce Bytes

A smaller site is a faster site! In general, reducing the size of the assets that need to be sent to the browser will be beneficial. There are several optimization tips, described in Chapter 6 and Chapter 7, that you can follow to slim down the assets of your page.

## Asset Checklist

▪ Minify your page assets such as HTML, CSS and JavaScript.

▪ Remember that images are your best friend, but also your worst enemy. The biggest optimization results can be achieved for images. Don't serve any more pixels than needed, by choosing the right image compression and format. Review the compression and format options discussed in Chapter 7.

- Measure the performance of your image format before settling on it. Use image formats such as PNG, GIF, JPEG, SVG or even encode the image into a base64 format (data URI) for the web.

- Avoid custom web fonts, using them only if really necessary. Where they are used, consider a web font loader, as discussed in Chapter 7.

- Use Gzip techniques, as introduced in Chapter 9, to reduce the file size sent over the wire.

# Reduce HTTP Requests

One of the important aspects of performance optimization is reducing the number of HTTP requests you make. Only serve the necessary files to the user. In order to achieve this, check out the following summarized tips, previously discussed in Chapter 5.

## Request Checklist

- Concatenate where applicable, to reduce the amount of HTTP requests. Be smart about it: separate more frequently changed code from less frequently changed code. Concatenate files based on these criteria, and use a more aggressive cache policy for the latter.

- "Less is more". Load only what matters, especially when using RWD.

- Don't blindly use JavaScript libraries and frameworks just because they are convenient.

- Use image sprites to reduce HTTP requests. Avoid too much white space between images to reduce memory consumption (see Chapter 5 for more details).

- For small images, consider using the data URI technique to remove additional HTTP requests.

# Fight Latency

Latency is the biggest bottleneck for lean websites, as discussed in Chapter 3, Chapter 5, Chapter 6, Chapter 7 and Chapter 9. Consider the steps below to lower latency as much as possible.

## Latency Checklist

- Measure your users' latency by using the Resource Timing API, as introduced in Chapter 3.

- Fight latency by reducing HTTP requests as much as possible (see "Reduce HTTP requests" above).

- The highest latency occurs on mobile devices. Additional latency is caused by the radio of the device, as discussed in Chapter 10 and Chapter 11.

- Reduce the amount of polling on your page. Don't constantly try to fetch new content in the background, especially if it's not immediately needed.

- Send the most important styles down the wire as soon as you can.

- Remove redirects where possible.

- Use the `keep-alive` header that keeps TCP connections open to reduce latency, as explained in Chapter 3 and Chapter 9.

- Use offline storage techniques such as appcache, local storage, Web SQL database, or IndexedDB to cut down on latency. Review Chapter 11 for more details.

- Use content delivery networks to avoid high latency, by moving requested resources closer to the users and thus reducing round trip time. Chapter 9 outlines further server quick wins.

- HTTP/2 (and formerly SPDY) provide efficient use of network resources and reduced latency, by allowing multiple concurrent requests on the same connection.

# Make Friends with the Server

You wouldn't believe how much a little *server love* can help your performance efforts. The examples in Chapter 9 show that with only a little bit of effort in server optimization—such as using Gzip compression—huge performance improvements can be made. The tips below recap the most important ones.

## Server Checklist

- Gzip uncompressed assets such as HTML, XML, JSON and CSS.

- Create a solid cache policy, as described in Chapter 9. Use conditional requests (content-based and time-based) to specify how to retrieve assets from the network.

- Consider PageSpeed Insights for your web server. It's a great tool for reducing some of the performance workload by applying `mod_pagespeed` filters.

# Tame the Mobile Beast

One of the biggest challenges of mobile web browsing is the latency that comes with the radio and wireless connections. Don't fear it, but be aware of it. Chapter 10 and Chapter 11 covered important aspects of mobile web performance, which are summarized below.

## Mobile Tips

- Be respectful of your visitors' data charges on mobile. Don't make the user pay for *your* bad performance.

- Avoid domain sharding (on mobile). More HTTP requests and DNS lookups will result in higher latency.

- Pay attention to RUM or Analytics data to understand your users' connection speed and latency, then optimize them.

- Weigh the advantages and disadvantages of different mobile strategies. Choose between mdot, RWD, RESS or RESS with ESI. Review Chapter 11 for a comparison table.

- Apply device description repositories to assist you with device detection.

- RESS with ESI redirect offers an additional advantage over regular server-side redirects: it occurs at the edge, and is faster than putting the redirect logic at the origin.

- Remove the need for a mobile direct by encouraging your user to bookmark your mdot site rather than using the desktop URL.

- Mobile devices are powered by batteries. Understand what causes the battery to drain: rendering images takes up most of the total rendering energy, followed by executing JavaScript code. Also, the more items are styled on a page, the bigger is the energy consumption for style sheets.

- Consider offline storage techniques as described in Chapter 11.

- Test your mobile experience on real devices, as much as possible.

# Automate Your Performance Routines

The idea behind automating performance optimization, as discussed in Chapter 8, is to help you build and maintain lean websites with the least manual labor. Using APIs and task runners to programmatically produce performant code during deployment helps greatly in producing lean websites.

## Automation Checklist

- Leverage the power of the PageSpeed Insights API to check for performance bottlenecks, apply filters and rules, and provide warnings. Review the list of filters in Chapter 8.

- Use task runners such as Grunt, Gulp, Maven or Ant—as discussed in Chapter 8—to make performance optimization a component of your deployment process.

- Even better, include task runners and performance APIs in your continuous integration system. Check out YSlow's continuous integration plugins, as introduced in Chapter 8.

# Stay in Shape and Avoid the Yo-yo Effect

Maintaining a lean website is a bit like following a weight loss program. It's all too common, after slimming down, to gain back all the weight lost in no time! As in dieting, so in maintaining lean websites, we need to avoid the yo-yo effect[4]. The monitoring tools discussed in Chapter 4, and the performance automation tools described in Chapter 8, help us to keep on top of website optimization.

## Monitoring Checklist

- Measure first, then optimize.

- Constant measuring and monitoring of your website's performance will help you identify performance bottlenecks and deal with them.

- Set up daily performance reports and warnings to keep your performance mind at ease.

- Automation can be incredibly helpful in fighting the yo-yo effect by triggering appropriate warnings. Review Chapter 8 for tools and options for keeping on top of this.

# Cool Down

This is our last cool down before the end of the book. I'd like to close this last chapter with a quote by Larry Page, the founder of Google:

> "Browsing should be as simple and fast as turning a page in a magazine."

May that inspire us all to aim for leaner websites!

---

[4] http://en.wikipedia.org/wiki/Yo-yo_effect

CPSIA information can be obtained at www.ICGtesting.com
Printed in the USA
BVOW09s1352210615

405510BV00009B/36/P